St. John (Gannow)
SCHOOL

❖

**Presented to**

Neil Tomlinson

Norman Hulme

JOHN R. AINSWORTH LTD., BURNLEY

A contrast in front ends at Crewe – steam Class '8P' 4-6-2 No. 71000 *Duke of Gloucester* and 25 kV a.c. electric locomotive No. E3001.

**From a painting by V. K. WELCH**

# TRAINS ANNUAL 1963

★English Electric Type '5' 3,300 h.p. diesel-electric No. D9009 *Alycidon* approaches Peterborough North with the up 'Flying Scotsman' on August 19, 1961. In the centre background is New England yard and on the right, behind the signal gantry, the new merchandise freight depot at Peterborough.

[*P. H. Wells*

# TRAINS ANNUAL 1963

Edited by
G. FREEMAN ALLEN

LONDON:
Ian Allan Ltd

# Contents

★Working on its diesel engine, Southern Region electro-diesel locomotive No. E6001 passes Winchester on a test run from Eastleigh to Basingstoke in February, 1962.                    [R. Puntis

# Early days with the Class 'A4' Pacifics

## by H. C. WEBSTER

★A July, 1937 view of Class 'A4' Pacifics on display outside Kings Cross shed. Reading from the left, the first four are all but one of those built for the 'Coronation' streamlined service; on the extreme right is No. 4482 *Golden Eagle*, the first built in green livery for ordinary East Coast Route express work. [British Railways

### ● The personal experiences of an L.N.E.R. locomotive man in the late 1930's.

PERHAPS it was not quite such a well-kept secret as the original 'Hush-Hush' engine of 1929, Gresley's water-tube-boilered, four-cylinder, No. 10000 of Class 'W1'. Nevertheless Gresley's Class 'A4' streamlined 4-6-2 design was kept very quiet. Whilst we of what was at that time the L.N.E.R. Locomotive Running Department knew that something of the sort was afoot, none of us had any idea of what a streamlined engine was going to look like.

I had personally visualized something very sleek and swift-looking – as straight and arrow-like in appearance as was practicable. The house I then occupied actually stood in the Kings Cross loco yard and it was a disappointment to me when, opening my door one morning, I got my first glimpse of No. 2509 *Silver Link*, which had come up from Doncaster works during the night and stood on the disposal pits. What disappointed me most, I think, was the kind of hump that marred the top line of the boiler

barrel, and the short-looking tender that gave the whole thing a squat, dumpy appearance, very far from anything remotely resembling an arrow. The front end of the Gresley non-streamlined Pacific, with its squat chimney, long smokebox and beautiful proportions was immeasurably more impressive and inspiring to me. The original 'Silver Jubilee' livery of French grey, too, was drab and uninteresting. Of course, this unenthusiastic first impression was later tempered, not only by the 'A4s'' outstanding performance on consistently high-speed duty day after day, but even more by their unsurpassed reliability in service.

It was the practice at Kings Cross depot to run in all engines fresh from Doncaster works on the 7.10 a.m. Cambridge, a moderately timed, fairly short trip that suited the purpose very well. No. 2509, after inspection by Sir Nigel Gresley and a select few, duly fell into line. It was accompanied by the District Inspector, but gave us no trouble at all, though in

★Class 'A4' 4-6-2 No. 4496 *Golden Shuttle* (now No. 60008 *Dwight D. Eisenhower*), one of two built for the 'West Riding Limited' service, climbs upgrade out of Hitchin on the last stage of its run to London with the up 'Silver Jubilee'.                          [*C. C. B. Herbert*

view of the task that lay ahead of it, it was very carefully nursed. After the 7.10 it worked a few trips to Peterborough and Grantham and was then tuned up and prepared for the Press trial trip of the 'Silver Jubilee', on which we intended to attain and hold, if possible, the 100-m.p.h. figure.

In the light of what followed this seems to have been a very modest ambition, but we were breaking new ground. True, it had already been done as far back as 1904 by Driver Clements with the 4-4-0 *City of Truro* on the Great Western 'Ocean Mail' special, and we had ourselves put Class 'A3' 4-6-2 No. 2750 *Papyrus*

up to 108 m.p.h. with 213 tons near Little Bytham during 'Silver Jubilee' trials in the previous March. However, this was to be a sustained effort, not just a burst of speed; it had to be if the 'Silver Jubilee' schedule was to be anything more than hopeful booking.

The trip was run on September 27, 1935, a fine day with a dry rail. No. 2509 *Silver Link* left Kings Cross at 2.26 p.m. hauling seven cars equal to 220 tons – say 230 with passengers – and with Driver A. J. Taylor, Fireman J. Luty and a headquarters inspector on the footplate. In the train were Sir Ralph Wedgwood, the General Manager; Sir Nigel Gresley, the Chief

Mechanical Engineer; Stephen Groom, the Locomotive Running Superintendent, with his assistant, C. H. M. Elwell; R. H. Thom, the Mechanical Engineer Southern Area; a legion of accredited timetakers, including the renowned Cecil J. Allen; and an even larger number of Press and publicity representatives.

That famous run has now been too often recounted to need any retelling here; the 100 m.p.h. figure was reached as the train approached Hitchin station and for the ensuing 25 miles the speed never fell below it until the check for the notorious Offord Curve, which we made much too late for the comfort – and even, as it seemed to us in our terror – the safety of those in the train, who were flung violently and, in retrospect, with an amusing disregard for protocol against the sides of the coaches. I landed, I remember, on the midriff of the somewhat portly R. H. Thom, always a rather dignified and austere gentleman, who thereafter was never quite able to forgive me. The highest speed reached – and that twice – was $112\frac{1}{2}$

m.p.h. The 70 miles between Wood Green and Fletton Junction, Peterborough, were covered at an average of 91.8 m.p.h., after which there was no more hair-raising negotiation of curves. Apart from anything else, we had caught up the 1.40 p.m. from Kings Cross as we approached Monkswood signalbox, near Little Bytham.

At Barkston we ran on to the curve and stopped for a while. Naturally, we carefully examined *Silver Link*. The left pony axlebox seemed dangerously hot both to myself and the Inspector, but Gresley without the least hesitation declared it to be perfectly all right for the return run. He added, however, that we were not to attempt any gallop down Stoke bank, where we had hoped to attain something really startling. Thus, a mere $84\frac{1}{2}$ m.p.h. was touched between Corby and Little Bytham and later Tempsford was passed at $89\frac{1}{2}$ m.p.h.

A pretty severe test and examination of No. 2509 was conducted the next day, but she had come through well. The pony box had cooled

★The up 'West Riding Limited' on Langley troughs, near Stevenage, with Class 'A4' 4-6-2 No. 4489 *Dominion of Canada* in charge, in October, 1938.

[C. C. B. Herbert

**Below:** This snapshot was specially taken by the author of the accompanying article as a guide for Gateshead depot, when this shed received its first Class 'A4' in 1935 and needed advice on how to lift the front end.          [*H. C. Webster*]

**Above:** Class 'A4' Pacific No. 2509 *Silver Link* is serviced in Kings Cross yard after arrival with the Newcastle–London 'Silver Jubilee'. Note the winding key inserted in the valance above the leading bogie to open the front of the streamlined casing for access to the smokebox.          [*P. Ransome-Wallis*]

off considerably on the run up and at 5.30 p.m. on September 30 the engine went away with the 'Silver Jubilee' on its first revenue-earning trip in splendid fettle. Back at the shed we were in constant touch with Control. Passing times at the major points *en route* were telephoned to us and we did not relax until arrival 'on time' at Newcastle was confirmed.

Because of its moderate loading I personally was never very much afraid of the 'Jubilee' except perhaps for one unknown factor – the problematical effect of sustained high speed on rotating, pin-trimmed bearings, such as connecting rod big ends and coupling rods. I thought then, and still do, that there must be a critical speed beyond which the entire contents of the oil reservoirs of these bearings, oil and pins alike, would become static under the influence of centrifugal force. Whether or not such conditions did ever obtain it was never possible to determine. Accurate measurements of the oil consumed in these particular bearings suggested that they did, but no traceable ill-

effects resulted, probably because the felt pad strips with which the bushes were fitted maintained an unbroken oil film during the period of suspended pin lubrication.

An additional cause for concern during these first few weeks was the need to keep No. 2509 in fit condition to handle both up and down trains continuously, until the remaining two of the class (there were four in all), Nos. 2511 *Quicksilver* and 2512 *Silver Fox*, reached us from Doncaster. This was a tall order. It meant a mileage accumulation at the rate of 2,680 a week, because the second 'A4', No. 2510 *Silver King*, had to stand at Newcastle as pilot for the up train; on very few occasions did it actually work the 'Jubilee'.

Incidentally, No. 2509's mileage upset all our schedules for periodical examinations, which at that time were arranged on a period as distinct from a mileage basis, and fresh ones had quickly to be evolved. On the prevailing period basis, for instance, the mileage between each examination of, say, No. 2509's connecting rod big ends, for which the interval was then three months, would have been no fewer than 32,160 had *Silver Link* continued to do the double trip daily. A special schedule of examinations based upon mileage was therefore introduced for engines working the 'Jubilee'. Later, in 1939, this was standardized for all high-speed trains powered from Kings Cross depot until they were cancelled at the outbreak of war. The schedule was elaborate and on the cautious side, but at the time that it was evolved, high-speed streamlined running was a new thing in this country; perhaps it may now be revealed that much more trouble was expected, particularly with overheated bearings, than in fact materialized.

Greater use might perhaps have been made of No. 2510, but the enginemen as well as those in charge at Kings Cross were reluctant to bring it into the working, since we were not responsible for its maintenance, which was carried out in the Newcastle district. The enginemen particularly were helpful in that they would never 'book' any repair work at Gateshead that might be so extensive as to require substitution of the pilot, No. 2510. However, on more than one occasion a chance so substantial was taken with No. 2509 that it had to be officially frowned upon. Eventually, of course, the remaining two 'A4s' reached us and some of No. 2509's load could be eased.

In due course the 'A4s' were multiplied in gratifying numbers for the 'Coronation', 'West Riding Limited', and East Coast express traffic generally. Among the first to arrive were the blue 'Dominions'. It was the custom to 'launch' these with a small ceremony at Kings Cross station, at which, after appropriate speech-making, the nameplates were disclosed by drawing apart short curtains. This task was accorded to an important Commonwealth official, usually the High Commissioner of the Dominion after which the engine was named; he then drove the 'A4' down to the starting signal at the end of the platform. On one such occasion the visitor was taken into the cab, introduced to the driver's seat, shown the regulator handle and told to pull it outwards, towards him. The regulator of a new Pacific was invariably a little tight in the gland and stiff to move and his first tug was ineffectual. 'Pull it hard', urged Gresley a little impatiently. So effective was his admonition that at the second attempt the handle came back with a snap, hard against the full-open quadrant stop.

The roar that went up from the chimney and the crash of the rods as they spun the wheels round in a stream of sparks stunned us. The engine was in full forward gear and, as it was carrying a good head of steam, the rest can be imagined. Surprisingly enough, the first to recover was the High Commissioner himself who, with a 'better-put-it-back-where-it-was' movement, decisively slammed the lever shut again. No harm was done, but on subsequent occasions the District Inspector used to take up his position on the fireman's side, armed with a wooden wedge which he unobtrusively slipped between the handle and the stop.

In the early days of 'A4' operation, interest in the novelty of the design and their striking exploits in service overshadowed some inconvenient features that became apparent as we got more used to them. The most serious was the inaccessibility of the motion because of the valances, which, in the first examples, extended down practically to axle centre-line, shrouding every bearing of importance. It is true that hand holes were provided, but they were much too small; and what we wanted to inspect never seemed to be in the right place at the right time. Moreover, the valances joined up through the footplate with the boiler cleading, the whole forming a hood which effectively trapped the heat. Some relief was later obtained by cutting slotted air vents, but this did not significantly decrease the heating. Ultimately, we succeeded in getting the valances removed altogether – though not in Gresley's time. He was indeed an autocrat on matters touching his designs, and although we always had to report on new types, so far as their maintenance was concerned, I do not ever remember very much resulting.

A somewhat similar hot-air trap was formed on the 'A4s' above the footplate, as a result of the rubber sheeting that joined the back edge of the cab roof to the tender front plate. This made working conditions for the enginemen almost intolerable on a hot day. Fortunately, the 'yaw' between engine and tender soon started a tear in the edge of the rubber which, possibly assisted by an exasperated driver's pen-knife or the blade of a fireman's shovel, quickly ran right across so that the sheeting hung down in two parts; it could then legitimately be removed altogether. Usually we had no replacement available in the stores: or, if we had, we could claim that we were too busy to put it on.

Though it could not be regarded as a defect in design, perhaps, the business of raising the front end casing in order to get at the smokebox

★The pictures on this page illustrate (**above**) the 'A4' appearance in 1935, 'Silver Jubilee' grey livery; and (**below**) in B.R. Brunswick green, Nos. 2510 *Quicksilver* (now No. 60015) and 60017 *Silver Fox*.                                    [*C. P. Walker*

was a considerable nuisance. This was done through the medium of a long screw and travelling nut; the screw was turned by a winding key similar to, though larger than, the starting handle of a car. In my day engine drivers were without equal in the gentle art of losing things – and may still be so. A good driver could be relied upon to lose anything from an eight-pint

★Another latter-day view of Class 'A4' No. 60017 *Silver Fox*, emerging from Gasworks Tunnel on the climb out of Kings Cross with the 10.52 a.m. to Leeds on August 12, 1961.                [*C. P. Walker*

oil bottle with the oil inside to a $\frac{3}{4}/\frac{7}{8}$ ring spanner. These casing keys presented them with a heaven-sent opportunity to exercise this unique ability. Consequently, whenever an 'A4' came on to the disposal pits, other activities had to be suspended immediately while a search was organized for a key to open the casing door. When somebody did appear a long time afterwards waving one triumphantly, the casing still had to be wound open – not a very long or arduous operation, perhaps, but one envied the man on the next pit who had only to swing open his smokebox door on its hinges. The shovel sweep, too, when clearing the smokebox ashes, was both longer and more awkward in the case of the 'A4' than of the other Pacifics, and working conditions more cramped.

The specific purpose of the 'A4' design, of course, was streamlined, high-speed working, and engines of the class were always booked for the 'Silver Jubilee' of 1935 and the 'Coronation' and 'West Riding Limited' of 1937. The 'Silver Jubilee' was an unqualified success from start to finish; but with the 'Coronation' some thought Gresley came near to over-reaching himself. He was certainly closer to disaster than many people ever knew.

At 330 tons the 'Coronation' train was far too heavy to run as a high-speed service and Edinburgh was too far away. In fact, the whole thing, during the time that I was at Kings Cross, was just a bit above the 'A4' – and ourselves as well. With no margin at all in which to get back a little lost time, just one signal check early on a bank meant a delay that was not to be recovered. True, this was a traffic man's problem; but what mattered to all of us was not the departmental responsibility but the late arrival. Just a hundredweight of poor coal, just a pinhole leak into the vacuum brake system – and the run became a heart-breaking struggle all the rest of the way, with certain defeat at the end of it.

In addition to all this, the 'Coronation' was, for some mysterious reason, what we used to call a 'dragger'; the train seemed to 'sit back' on the drawbar like a reluctant dog on its collar. Three hundred and thirty tons may be a fixed weight, but any engineman will confirm that whereas one train of that weight may run freely and feel like 200, another will drag and feel like 600. There are several reasons for this, among them the consumption of electric current, all of which has to be generated by axle-driven dynamos, and in the case of the 'Coronation' this was pretty considerable.

Yet another factor that handicapped the 'Coronation' when compared with the 'Jubilee' was the changing of enginemen *en route*. This meant divided responsibility for operation as well as maintenance, a thing we avoided at all costs in the case of the 'Jubilee', whose enginemen would, of their own accord, limp home somehow or other rather than let any other depot so much as tighten a $\frac{7}{8}$-in. bolt.

Gresley himself was very concerned about the running of the 'Coronation'. I have often watched him – although from a safe distance – pacing the arrival platform at 10.30 p.m.: and pacing it ever more anxiously as the minutes overdue steadily mounted. When at last the train did come in he spoke a few words to the driver, nodded his head gravely and left.

The 'West Riding Limited', third of this once-famous trio, passed almost unnoticed, overshadowed by the other two. Although it was as heavy as the 'Coronation' its journey of 186 miles was, by comparison, negligible and we took this working in our stride.

It was always my own personal opinion that the most successful performance put up by these early 'A4s', with the possible exception of the 'Jubilee' workings, was on the Kings Cross–Edinburgh non-stop 'Flying Scotsman'. This was a gruelling test of both engine and enginemen and, for that matter, of the entire organization behind the job. The 'Jubilee' was faster – quite a bit faster – but it was also lighter, often no more than half the weight. The 'Coronation' was as fast, but that too was lighter and there

were intermediate stops – stops of only a matter of minutes, it is true, but with luck, long enough to slip on a pilot and get away with it.

With the 'non-stop' there was no safety margin at all; once away from No. 10 platform the train must keep on running until it reached Edinburgh, all but 400 miles away. Six and a half hours used to seem an appalling time for any locomotive to maintain such near-maximum output without a break. So many unforeseen things could happen during that time which could stop it, and a day rarely passed without an anxious glance at the office clock and an unspoken prayer that she might be nearly there by now. Sometimes things did happen to stop the train, of course. In fact, in only one of the seven seasons that I was at Kings Cross did it get through without a single involuntary stop, although I cannot remember one that was the direct result of engine failure.

Water supplies were always our biggest risk. Any one of the six troughs between London and Edinburgh – Langley, Werrington, Muskham, Scrooby, Wiske Moor or Lucker – might be sluggish in refilling, following a dip by a late-running man in front; or the adjustment of the scoop might be the fraction of an inch out. The 'A4s' never carried less than eight tons of coal on this working. This load brought the snout of the water scoop hard down on to the gauge and left us the choice either of letting the engine go out with it set too low and liable to foul the trough, or too high, so that as the fuel load lightened *en route*, a full dip would not be taken at the last trough. Once over Lucker troughs we always reckoned that the 'non-stop' was out of danger.

It was with this train that 'A4' No. 4492 *Dominion of New Zealand* created something of a record during the summer of 1937 by running every trip throughout the season with the exception of three only. Such consistently reliable running was the direct result of a new system of booking out engines that the coming of the 'A4' to Kings Cross made possible. Until then, particular engines were always allocated to particular drivers. Many readers will associate the white-tyred No. 4472 *Flying Scotsman* with the famous Bill Sparshatt; a few of the older ones possibly remember No. 4472 as the engine of Ben Glasgow, from whom Sparshatt inherited it. I combine No. 2750 *Papyrus* with Guttridge, one of the most competent top link drivers ever at Kings Cross, No. 4476 *Royal*

(*Concluded on page* 39)

# A CUNEO PAINTING TAKES SHAPE

★ On this and the following page we illustrate some of the stages in the superb painting of Clapham Junction by Terence Cuneo which is reproduced on the jacket and inside this book. Mr. Cuneo is himself seen at work on the painting at the head of the page.

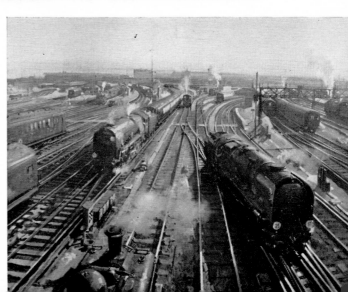

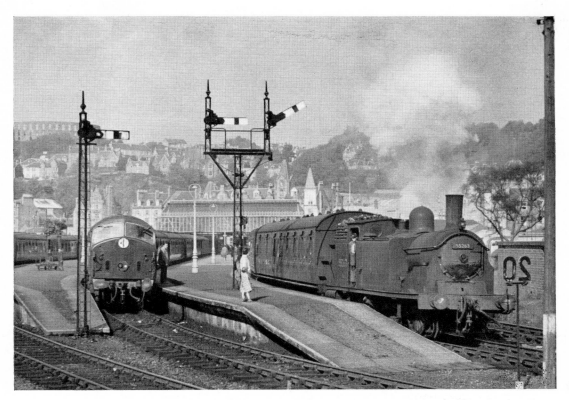

# The Callander and Oban Line

## by DAVID BERTRAM

★Oban terminus on May 13, 1961. Former Caledonian 0-4-4T No. 55263 leaves with the 4.55 p.m. to Balla-chulish; on the left is the 5.15 p.m. to Glasgow, headed by N.B. Loco. Co. Type 2 diesels Nos. D6135 and D6108.                    [M. Mensing

● A tour in text and picture of
one of Scotland's scenic routes

THE single track which branches sharply away from the Glasgow–Perth main line as it swings across the Allan Water immediately north of Dunblane station may not appear to be the beginning of an 82-mile branch; but after passing through some of the finest scenery in Britain, the single track terminates that distance away on the Scottish west coast at Oban. The Callander and Oban line, with its fine views of mountains and lochs, rivals the more publicized West Highland line for scenic attraction; and it is small wonder that the first observation car to run on British railways went into regular service on it.

Although it is usually referred to as the Callander and Oban line, in fact two separate companies were involved in the construction of the route. The first 11 miles from Dunblane were opened on July 1, 1858, within two years of being authorized by the Dunblane, Doune & Callander Railway. The line was worked from the beginning by the Scottish Central Railway and then by the Caledonian Railway when the former was taken over by the latter in 1865. Until the extension to the west was begun 12 years later, this section was known as the Callander branch. The Callander & Oban Railway was incorporated in 1865 and was the first railway to penetrate the previously impregnable Highlands from east to west. In 1870 the 18 miles between Callander and Glenogle-head were opened, making an end-on junction with the branch from Dunblane approximately ¾-mile east of Callander at what is now known as Callander & Oban Junction; the older line's separate terminus and the short section leading to it were then closed.

Over-expenditure on the next section to Tyndrum, 16 miles, resulted in financial embarrassment for the C.O.R. and the abandonment of the projected continuation westwards to Oban. However, the Caledonian Railway, already in possession of a line to Callander, came to the aid of the distressed company and in 1873 powers were again sought to continue to Oban. These were granted in 1874 and six years later, on July 1, 1880, the whole length was opened to through traffic. Within two years half of the visitors to Oban were travelling by rail. The C.O.R. remained nominally independent until the 1923 grouping, although the Caledonian Railway held a large percentage of the shares and was responsible for the working from its opening. The 82-mile branch thus took 22 years to complete.

From the junction on Dunblane bank the branch runs due west towards Doune through rolling grassland country, over easy curves with few gradients. Until 1955 the 4 miles between Dunblane and Doune were double track. Why this section of the original branch to Callander was made double track and the remaining 7 miles single is a mystery – one must assume

that the funds were insufficient to carry on in such a lavish way. Gradually the pastureland gives way to wilder country, and as the line runs farther north-westwards towards Callander into the valley of the River Teith the high land encroaches on both sides. Ahead, it seems impassable.

The approach to Callander is heralded by the now disused remains of the once-familiar ticket platform. The neat station, situated on a curve, is a well-known starting point for the Trossachs; it is sometimes referred to as the 'Gateway to the Highlands'.

The term 'Gateway to the Highlands' can well be applied to the railway, for within a very short distance of Callander it begins to trace a winding course from valley to valley, seeking the lowest possible route through the mountains. After crossing the River Leny it begins a climb at 1 in 50 through overhanging tree-covered slopes in the Pass of Leny. Ben Ledi (2,873 ft) overlooks the line as it emerges from the Pass. Twice within a very short distance the line crosses the River Leny again on low girder bridges. Past the loop at St Brides there is a remarkable transition to the calm and quiet of Loch Lubnaig. The line follows its south shore over level track to Strathyre, a village 20 miles from Dunblane at the head of the water, and whose station – a passing loop – is celebrated for its well-kept appearance. A further short stretch over level ground through country made famous in Sir Walter Scott's novel *Rob Roy*

Callander station, looking in the Oban direction, with a diesel multiple-unit on a 'Six Lochs' land cruise from Glasgow at the platform in April, 1961.

[*S. Rickard*

Former Caledonian Railway Class '2P' 0-4-4T No. 55124 climbs out of Oban with the 4.55 p.m. to Balla-chulish on May 18, 1961.

A pair of North British Loco. Type '2' diesel-electric locomotives, Nos. D6135 and D6108, start the 5.15 p.m. to Glasgow and Edin-burgh out of Oban station on May 13, 1961.

**Photographed by**
**M. MENSING**

The down afternoon 'Birmingham Pullman' of the Western Region arrives at Solihull on May 31, 1961.

English Electric Type '4' diesel-electric No. D314 west of Brinklow, on the Trent Valley main line, with the 4.5 p.m. Euston–Blackpool on August 6, 1961.

**Photographed by**
**M. MENSING**

★Another view of Callander station, with a midday departure for Glasgow headed by Class '5' 4-6-0 No. 45357. The station's once dominant feature has now gone. Surmounting an enclosed overbridge was a clock tower, but in 1948 several wagons of a westbound freight broke away and ran back into the station to collide with a Glasgow train, badly damaging the overbridge.
[R. E. Toop

leads to Kingshouse Halt and then follows a short rise before Balquhidder.

Balquhidder is one of the most important stations on the branch. It is situated between the villages of Balquhidder and Lochearnhead and until the opening of the line from Crieff in 1893 was known as Lochearnhead. This branch, however, was closed to all traffic on October 1, 1951, and subsequently lifted. The station consists of an up island platform and a narrow down platform, together with a number of sidings. Steam locomotives generally take water at Balquhidder, for beyond this passing point there is a tremendous climb.

Immediately after the restart from Balquhidder past the junction of the Crieff line, the climb begun just before the station is continued in earnest. The next $5\frac{1}{4}$ miles are at a ruling gradient of 1 in 60 to the summit at Glenoglehead, 940 ft above sea-level. As the train is lifted up the hillside, magnificent scenery unfolds below. There is the full length of Loch Earn, the village of Lochearnhead and the remains of the line to Crieff, with its fine viaduct. As the climb continues the vegetation thins out and is quite sparse near the summit. The views disappear as the train approaches Glenoglehead, 28 miles from Dunblane, where the original platforms used when this point was the terminus of the line between 1870 and 1886 still survive; then known as Killin, it now serves as a passing loop where train crews change their mounts.

Once clear of the summit the line falls sharply for the first time since leaving the main line. Speed is restrained on the 1 in 69 down through the bare rocks of the twisting Glen Ogle to Killin Junction, an exchange platform on a bleak open hillside. There is no road access and this small station closely resembles the better-known Riccarton Junction on the Waverley route. Here one can look across Killin to the head of Loch Tay and in clear weather see also the mighty Ben Lawers beyond. Killin Junction is the terminus of the short, sharply-graded 4-mile branch to Killin, opened in 1886. Until September, 1939, the Killin branch continued to Loch Tay, but now it serves only the small but popular resort of Killin.

Westwards from Killin Junction, the descent continues down the bare hillside into Glen Dochart. Through Luib the gradient levels out and speed increases, but rounded mountains continue to dominate a wild and bare scene; Ben More (3,843 ft) can be seen towering over the lower hills. Two small lochs relieve this bleak prospect, but even in midsummer one can usually discern snow in the gullies on the northern slopes of Ben More.

Forty miles from Dunblane is Crianlarich. This small hamlet of 400 people has the distinction of being served by two separate lines, thanks to its situation at the head of Strath Fillan, Glen Dochart and Glen Falloch. Here the Oban line passes beneath the West Highland line as the latter leaves the Crianlarich Upper

★Class '5' 4-6-0 No. 45099 threads the pass of Leny and approaches Callander with an Oban–Glasgow train on August 6, 1957.

[W. S. Sellar

★Class '5' 4-6-0 No. 45157 *The Glasgow Highlander* crosses the River Teith near the Falls of Leny, north of Callander, with an evening train for Oban in June, 1958.

[W. J. V. Anderson

★North British Loco. Co. Type 2 diesels Nos. D6101 and D6127 skirt Loch Lubnaig, between Strathyre and Callander, with the now withdrawn 12.5 p.m. Oban–Glasgow Buchanan Street train on August 12, 1961.

[W. A. C. Smith

★Another view of Loch Lubnaig, with the Callander–Oban line skirting the opposite shore. The train photographed on July 23, 1961 was a nine-car formation of diesel multiple-units making the 'Six Lochs' land cruise from Coatbridge.

[S. Rickard

Balquhidder station in May, 1957. Two Class '5' 4-6-0s stand at the platform with a photographers' excursion organised by British Railways from Glasgow to Killin and back.

[British Railways

**Left:** Ex-Caledonian Railway 0-4-4T No. 55263 climbs Glenogle with the 4.5 p.m. school train from Callander to Killin in May, 1960. [*W. J. V. Anderson*

**Below:** Another view in Glenogle in May, 1960, with Class '5' 4-6-0 No. 45084 making the ascent on an Oban-bound freight train. [*W. J. V. Anderson*

(*Continued from page* 17)
station to cross the Fillan Water and follow the eastern slopes of the wide Strath Fillan to Tyndrum. The Oban line is joined by a spur from the Upper station approximately half a mile beyond its own Lower station. Opened on August 7, 1894, when the W.H.R. was opened beyond Craigendoran, this steeply graded double-track spur has seen little traffic, apart from freight and excursions. Until 1962 the only regular service to use it was a short-lived buffet-car train between Glasgow Queen Street and Oban. The 1962 summer timetable, however, introduced a new weekday service from Glasgow Queen Street at 9.35 a.m. to Oban, reached at 12.50 p.m., with a return working at 5.15 p.m. regaining Glasgow at 8.30 p.m.; designed for tourist travel, it is formed of diesel multiple-unit stock with mini-buffet facilities.

Beyond Crianlarich the Oban line climbs the opposite slopes of Strath Fillan parallel with the West Highland line. For 4 miles these lines are in full view of each other, but their services are so infrequent that it is rare indeed to see a train on each simultaneously. From Crianlarich the gradient is relatively easy at first, but approaching Tyndrum it steepens to 1 in 44. As at Crianlarich, the C.O.R. station at Tyndrum is known as the 'Lower' and was for four years the terminus of the line, during which time the village regained some of its former importance as a coaching station at the confluence of the routes to Oban and Fort William. The original terminus is the seemingly oversized goods yard on the up side of the line at a slightly lower level. Nowadays, Tyndrum Lower's main importance is as a passing loop.

The steep climb continues at 1 in 49 from Tyndrum until the line crosses the watershed and begins a steep descent, mainly at 1 in 55, through Glen Lochy. In the distance ahead can be seen the mighty Ben Cruachan. For eastbound trains this climb is the hardest part of the whole route. Dalmally is the next station of importance, $46\frac{1}{4}$ miles from Callander, and here steam locomotives usually take water again before setting off across the River Orchy. Soon the line reaches the foot of Loch Awe and passengers enjoy a good view of the ruined island castle of Kilchurn. In this area there is some of the finest scenery of the whole route, with the wide expanse of Loch Awe stretching away to the south-west and Ben Cruachan now close at hand.

Loch Awe station, $2\frac{1}{2}$ miles from Dalmally,

is well situated on the side of the loch. Adjacent to the white-painted, two-platform station with passing loop is a pier from which summer excursions by the M.V. *Countess of Breadalbane* were initiated in 1936, suspended in 1939 and reintroduced in 1948. A reminder of the industrial developments in the Highlands is the number of bulk cement wagons usually to be found in the goods yard; they supply the Loch Awe hydro-electric scheme.

The line skirts the northern shore of the loch and at its western end follows the waters into the narrow Pass of Brander. As the extensive views to the south disappear the climb begins again, but less steeply than on previous occasions, at 1 in 100. Through the steep-sided pass past the Falls of Cruachan platform the line continues upwards, apparently clinging to the southern slopes of Ben Cruachan, high above the swift-flowing River Awe. Because of the danger of falling rocks, 14 automatic stone signals were installed many years ago on this stretch. They are interconnected by wires strung across the hillside above the track and are normally in the 'off' position. Falling rock or stones break the wires, whereupon the signals return to 'danger'; at the same time a warning bell rings in the signalbox and neighbouring linesmen's cottages. On August 8, 1946, a huge rock bounced *over* the wires on to the track and the 6.5 a.m. Oban–Glasgow, headed by a Stanier Class '5' 4-6-0, was derailed, with several coaches overhanging the river 100 ft below. This danger has resulted in the imposition of a severe speed restriction on all trains through the Pass, especially at night.

Beyond the Pass of Brander, more open country is reached again at Taynuilt, 69 miles from Dunblane. Here the surrounding hills are much lower, the countryside has some use for cattle-grazing and there is an air of greater activity. Now follow short and frequent changes of gradients with numerous brief cuttings. To the north, Loch Etive has come into view and beyond it are the hills of Benderloch. Beyond Taynuilt the line runs closer towards and eventually alongside Loch Etive to Ach-na-Cloich ($72\frac{1}{2}$ miles from Dunblane) and Connel Ferry, the last station – and junction – before Oban. Shortly after leaving Ach-na-Cloich station one can see the Connel Ferry bridge carrying the branch to Ballachulish across the foot of the loch.

The $27\frac{1}{2}$-mile branch to Ballachulish runs north across the Loch, through Benderloch and

Appin to the shores of Loch Leven. Opened in 1903, it was intended to reach Fort William and ultimately Inverness. Its junction is immediately west of Connel Ferry station. Originally, there was to have been a triangular layout to enable trains to run directly on to this line from both directions, but although some earthworks and a bridge were completed the approach from the Oban direction was never laid. Thus trains

climb in its 82-mile course. For three miles the grade is at 1 in 50 to the summit at Glencruiten, 301 ft above sea-level. Beyond the passing loop at the summit there is a similar fall for 3 miles to sea-level at Oban. During the later stages of this descent the line makes a complete turn to approach the town from the south, offering magnificent views of Oban Bay and Mull beyond as a finale to the journey.

★A view from the 6.5 a.m. Oban–Glasgow and Edinburgh train as North British Locomotive Co. Type 2 diesels Nos. D6123 and D6102 approach Glenlochy crossing on May 20, 1961.                     [M. Mensing

coming from the Oban direction – as most of the branch services do – must reverse in Connel Ferry station, where there is a fairly extensive layout, with a down side island platform and a bay at each end of the up platform, as well as several sidings.

From Connel Ferry the Oban line swings south-west and runs inland to make the last

Approaching the town the line runs past the former ticket platform used until 1939 and the small motive power depot and fairly large yard behind it on the right-hand side before threading a deep double-track cutting to emerge at the harbour side and terminate in the spacious station.

Traffic on the Callander & Oban line is

★Another view of the wild terrain in the neighbourhood of Glenogle. Two Class '5' 4-6-0s are tackling the gradient with an Oban–Glasgow train in August, 1954.
[J. Woolfenden

★The beaver-tail observation car of the pre-war London–Edinburgh 'Coronation' streamliner brings up the rear of the 5.15 p.m. Oban–Glasgow Buchanan Street as it passes Crianlarich East Junction on July 20, 1957. Diverging to the right is the spur connecting with the West Highland line, which can be seen crossing the valley on a viaduct in the centre background.
[W. A. C. Smith

★Class '4F' 0-6-0 No. 44318 pauses for steam just short of Tyndrum station on an Oban-bound freight.
[W. J. V. Anderson

**Left:** Class '5' 4-6-0 No. 45473 leaves Tyndrum with the midday train from Glasgow to Oban in May, 1955. The West Highland line follows the upper layer of trees on the left-hand side of the picture.

[W. J. V. Anderson

**Below left:** The 12 noon Glasgow–Oban train emerges from the Pass of Brander in May, 1960 behind Class '5' 4-6-0 No. 44880. In the centre of the picture is one of the automatic rock-fall signals for which this section of the route is famous.     [M. Mensing

**Above:** A view from an Oban–Glasgow train approaching Awe crossing in May, 1961; on the right are the works of the Loch Awe hydro-electric project.

[M. Mensing

**Left:** The morning Glasgow and Edinburgh–Oban train climbs away from Taynuilt in May, 1960 headed by Class '5' 4-6-0 No. 45482. The distant peak is Ben Cruachan.

[M. Mensing

heavier than on its neighbour, the West High-land. Owing to the variations in gradients between up and down directions the normal loading for passenger trains headed by an unaided Class '5' 4-6-0 has been eight coaches eastbound and six coaches westbound. Consequently, there is an unequal number of up and down trains – four and five respectively on weekdays in the 1961/62 winter timetable, which is the one current at the time of writing. The down trains depart from Stirling at 12.12 (with through coach leaving Glasgow at 10.30 p.m.) and 6 a.m. and Buchanan Street at 7.50 a.m., 12 noon and 6 p.m. The 12.12 a.m. arrives in Oban at 5.7 a.m. and carries mainly parcels and mail; it does not run during the summer. The 6 a.m. from Stirling has a connection from Glasgow Central at the unearthly hour of 4 a.m. and on Saturday mornings the sleeping-cars off the 7.15 p.m. from Euston are transferred to this train at Stirling. Until late September one of the ex-'Devon Belle' observation cars is attached to the rear of the 7.50 a.m. and at Callander through coaches are added from Edinburgh Princes Street to Oban, where arrival is at 12.28 p.m. The 6 p.m. from Buchanan Street, due in Oban at 9.58 p.m., attaches at Stirling through coaches from Edinburgh Princes Street, which is left at 5.30 p.m. Until January, 1961, the evening service to Oban departed from Buchanan Street at 5.15 p.m., arriving in Oban at 9.35 p.m. However, the 5.15 p.m. departure was made a semi-fast service to Callander only and the 6 p.m. introduced as a new express to Stirling, giving an acceleration of 23 min. Edinburgh passengers benefited even more, for instead of departing at 4.16 p.m. they now leave at 5.30 p.m. and enjoy an overall reduction in journey time of 52 min.

In the up direction there is no overnight service, the first departure being at 6.5 a.m. from Oban, due in Glasgow at 10.28 a.m. and Edinburgh at 11.14 a.m. Other trains also convey through coaches to both Glasgow and Edinburgh; the 12.5 p.m. reaches Glasgow at 4.22 p.m. and Edinburgh at 4.43 p.m., and the 5.15 p.m. from Oban is due in the two cities at 9.25 p.m. and 9.56 p.m. respectively. The 5.15 p.m. is an important and heavy train, for in addition to parcels and mail traffic it carries on Mondays only the sleeping-cars for Euston and the observation car when the latter is in service; the sleeping cars are detached at Stirling and added to the 9 p.m. Perth–Euston train. In the 1961/62 winter, one train each way – the 12

noon from Glasgow and 9.30 p.m. from Oban – was withdrawn as an economy measure; the down train only carried an Edinburgh portion.

Journey times are relatively slow. The 117 miles between Glasgow and Oban require a minimum of 3 hr. 58 min. by the 6 p.m. down and a maximum of 6 hr. 37 min. by the over-night train. The fastest up service, the 9.30 a.m. ex-Oban, takes 4 hr. 9 min. On the C.O.R. section the nine trains call at almost all stations, the only exceptions being Kingshouse and Ach-na-Cloich, which are served by certain trains provided notice is given. Between Callander and Glasgow, however, these services range from ones calling only at Stirling, such as the 6 p.m. down, to semi-fasts with five stops. Trains to the Oban line not booked to call at Dunblane run via the down branch platform line.

During the summer, when tourist traffic greatly expands the number of trains on the line, this service is augmented. During the 1961 summer timetable period there was a through train on Friday nights from Euston arriving in Oban at 8.7 a.m., conveying throughout the sleepers sent forward on the 6 a.m. from Stirling on other weekdays and reliefs to both the 7.50 a.m. and 12 noon down trains. In the up direction the 12.5 p.m. was relieved by a train to Glasgow at 11.35 a.m. and Edinburgh at 12.45 p.m., whilst the 5.15 p.m. up had a relief at 6 p.m. on weekdays and 6.35 p.m. on Satur-days, these latter conveying the sleeping cars. These additional summer trains made only a limited number of intermediate halts on the C.O.R. line, but due to frequent tablet ex-changes and waits to cross other trains they showed little reduction in overall journey times.

The Sunday service no longer exists, as the 7.35 a.m. from Glasgow has been withdrawn from the current timetable. No return service has ever existed. In the summer of 1957, when the Scottish Region introduced a number of additional Sunday services, the Oban line had a 10.35 a.m. down, returning from Oban at 6.10 p.m., but these trains were short-lived and disappeared in the economy drive of July, 1958. Excursions, of which more will be written later, are the only other trains on Sundays.

Callander is the terminal for a number of trains. These are also weekdays-only services and originate mainly from Glasgow or Stirling, but there is an 8.48 a.m. (SX) arrival from Edinburgh Princes Street which includes a through coach for Oban (the latter has a 45-min.

wait at Callander). One afternoon service is provided by a diesel multiple-unit, due at 3.39 p.m.; this and the return service at 4 p.m. are the only regular working by such units on the Oban line. In the up direction the pattern is similar, including a 9.40 a.m. (SX) to Edinburgh.

So far as the C.O.R. is concerned, the first sign of nationalization was the introduction of a daily through train from Glasgow Queen Street to Oban via the West Highland line to Crianlarich and the connecting spur to the Oban line at this point. It was a five-coach buffet-car set which departed from Queen Street at 9.31 a.m. and reached Oban at 1.15 p.m., giving a journey time of only 3 hr. 44 min., whilst the return service at 6.25 p.m. from Oban was even faster, reaching Glasgow at 9.55 p.m. in 3½ hr. flat. This service proved a white elephant. Despite the distance being 16 miles less than via Stirling and the fact that the Oban Town Council had asked for this routing, the trains did not attract sufficient patronage to justify more than a brief reinstatement after 1949. The train was worked throughout in each direction by an Eastfield Class B1 4-6-0.

Passenger services on the Oban line's two branches are run in connection with the Oban services. Between Killin Junction and Killin there are five trains in each direction provided by the branch locomotive and its single second class, non-corridor coach. Only the overnight train from Glasgow has no connecting service to Killin, but as this calls at Killin Junction at 2.10 a.m. it is hardly surprising. Until two years ago there was a late Saturday evening service from Killin at 8.25 p.m. to Callander, returning thence at 9.58 p.m. There is still an unadvertised service for the benefit of schoolchildren who have used the 6.5 a.m. from Oban in the morning to reach Callander. The Killin branch locomotive runs to Callander to head a 4.6 p.m. from Callander to Luib, where it hands over the coach to the afternoon freight train from Stirling. The latter then runs as a mixed train to Crianlarich, whilst the Killin branch locomotive runs back to Killin Junction to resume its duties. The Ballachulish branch trains are three each way daily, with one extra each way on Saturdays; of these, there are two each way through to Oban. These branch trains connect with the Oban line trains at Connel Ferry and usually consist of two or three non-corridor coaches.

Several features of the passenger timetables deserve further comment. The sleeping-car services, now provided by B.R. standard vehicles, have had a chequered career during the past few years. During the winter months they are run only once weekly in each direction, from Euston on Friday evenings and back from Oban on Mondays. In summer they are run daily from Sundays to Fridays northbound and Mondays to Saturdays southbound.

Dining car services were introduced by the Caledonian Railway when Pullman restaurant cars were put to work on Glasgow–Oban trains. These services have continued. The ex-C.R. Pullman cars continued in use after 1923 and when the Pullman contract with the L.M.S.R. ended in 1933 the 20 cars in use on the Oban, Caledonian and Highland sections were repainted in L.M.S. livery and staffed by L.M.S. crews. These cars have been replaced by modern vehicles only in the past few years. At present restaurant-car facilities are offered on only one train in each direction; one car based on Oban makes a round trip to Glasgow on the 12.5 p.m. up and 6 p.m. down. It is interesting to note that a spare car is held at Oban, yet when a changeover is necessary a third car arrives, when one would have thought that by prior arrangement the cars could be changed over at Glasgow. During the summer months an additional service is provided by a Glasgow-based car on the 12 noon from Buchanan Street and the 6 p.m. (SX) or 6.37 p.m. (SO) back.

The original observation car on this line, *Maid of Morven*, was an adapted eight-wheeled vehicle built by Cravens of Sheffield in 1914. It was introduced to the C.O.R. in the summer of 1923. In addition to the armchair observation section, there were two compartments and a small kitchen. For many years this car was attached to the 9.45 a.m. down and 3.35 p.m. up. The car was first class only and no supplementary charges were made. After its withdrawal in 1937 no observation cars ran until 1957, when one of the cars from the withdrawn 'Devon Belle' Pullman train was repainted in B.R. maroon livery, renumbered Sc281M, and transferred to the Scottish Region. It now runs during the summer on the 7.55 a.m. from Glasgow and the 5.15 p.m. from Oban; it was also attached to the rear of the short-lived Sunday service. A supplementary charge is made now, but at 3s. 6d. for the whole journey is inexpensive. A small kitchen at the inner end of the car enables valuable light refreshments (*Continued on page* 31)

**Right:** A pair of North British Locomotive Co. Type '2' diesels, Nos. D6102 and D6123, negotiate the curves down from Glencruiten crossing in May, 1961 with the 12 noon Glasgow–Oban.  [*M. Mensing*

**Below:** Another view on the descent from Glencruiten crossing to Connel Ferry; an up freight is headed by Class '5' 4-6-0 No. 45159 in May, 1960.  [*M. Mensing*

**Left:** Former Caledonian Railway Class '2F' 0-6-0 No. 57441 stands at Killin Junction after arrival with the Killin branch train on April 27, 1961.   [N. A. Machell

# BRANCHES OF THE OBAN LINE

**Below:** With the massif of Ben Lawers in the background, 0-4-4T No. 55263 sets out for Killin Junction with the 1.42 p.m. from Killin in May, 1960.

[W. J. V. Anderson

**Above:** A 'Six Lochs' diesel multiple-unit land cruise from the Glasgow area at Killin station on April 3, 1961.

*[S. Rickard*

**Right:** Ex-Caledonian 0-4-4T No. 55263 simmers outside the Killin branch shed on the shores of Loch Tay on August 23, 1961. *[A. R. Butcher*

**Below:** Class '2F' 0-6-0 No. 57246 soon after leaving Killin Junction with the 2.46 p.m. to Killin in August, 1959.

*[J. C. Beckett*

**Above:** A down fitted freight of Presflo alumina wagons for the British Aluminium Co. at Kinlochleven via Ballachulish approaches Connel Ferry, on the shores of Loch Etive, behind Class '5' 4-6-0 No. 45163 in May, 1960. In the right background is Connel Ferry bridge. [M. Mensing

**Right:** An afternoon train to Oban leaves Ballachulish behind 0-4-4T No. 55208 in May, 1955. [W. J. V. Anderson

(*Continued from page* 26)
to be served, as on this long journey there is only one refreshment room, at Callander. One hopes that soon some of the new miniature buffet-cars, now so numerous in Scotland, will be allocated to the Oban trains.

Over the years there have been few basic changes in the passenger services. In 1924, for instance, there were trains from Glasgow at 4.15 a.m., 8.0 a.m., 9.45 a.m., 12.10 p.m. and 5.10 p.m. The 9.45 a.m. had the observation car attached and the 5.10 p.m. the dining car. From Oban there were departures at 5.40 a.m., 9.10 a.m., 11.15 a.m., 11.50 a.m., 3.35 p.m. and 5.15 p.m. At the turn of the century the Scottish railways were endeavouring to stimulate long summer weekends away from the large cities, and amongst other services introduced to foster this traffic was the Caledonian's 'C. & O. Hotel Express', which left Glasgow on the Friday evening for Oban and returned on the following Monday morning; this service lasted from July, 1905, until September, 1911.

During the summer months a source of considerable revenue is the excursion traffic, and here the railway authorities have fully exploited the scenic grandeur of this route and the Western Isles. In addition to day excursions from the various Scottish centres there is a regular programme of excursions from English centres. From Glasgow, Edinburgh, Perth, Dundee and other smaller towns there are regular excursions, especially at holiday times and at weekends. In the past these trains, loaded to 12 corridor vehicles, often with full dining-car facilities, have proved a stiff task even for two locomotives. Whenever possible, they were routed over the C.O.R. one way and returned from Crianlarich over the West Highland line. Shorter-distance excursions were run up the West Highland and returned over the C.O.R. without traversing the Crianlarich–Oban section.

Their post-war successors have not normally had such heavy loads, nor have restaurant cars been attached on public excursions. The suitability of diesel multiple-units for sightseeing was quickly realized and now an ambitious programme utilizes up to eight-car trains each summer. Included in these activities are the popular 'Six Lochs Land Cruises', which follow the C.O.R., including the Killin branch, to Crianlarich and return over the West Highland line or vice versa. The longer-distance excursions, usually from England, are run in conjunction with the steamers of David MacBrayne Ltd. from Oban. After an overnight journey, on which sleeping cars are often available in addition to a buffet car, a full day is spent on the steamer, usually visiting Staffa and Iona before returning to Oban for an overnight return journey. From Euston, for instance, such an excursion was run annually in the late 1930s for 70s. These excursions still run and one in 1960 originated from Sheffield and Leeds; in 1961 an excursion came from East Anglia. The summer excursions on Loch Awe with the M.V. *Countess of Breadalbane* were served for a number of years by a train to and from Oban, but this has been withdrawn. For the more individualistic tastes, there is a 25s. Holiday Runabout Ticket which gives a week's unlimited travel on the C.O.R. between Callander and Oban and also between Crianlarich and Fort William.

Freight traffic, naturally, is not heavy. In an area of such small population with virtually no industries, the freight traffic which does exist is mainly of a general nature. There are two sources of heavier traffic, however. One is temporary – the supply of cement in bulk to the hydro-electric works on Loch Awe; the other is the container traffic to the railhead at Ballachulish for transport by road to Kinlochleven. Aluminium oxide is conveyed for smelting at the British Aluminium Co. plant in this remote part of Scotland and up to 20 wagons daily have been required for this traffic.

At present there are two trains each way daily for the regular traffic, but special freight trains are often required for cattle, etc. All trains are Class K and call as required at stations on the line. In the down direction departures from Central Yard at Stirling are at 6.15 a.m. and 1.35 p.m.; both trains take between eight and nine hours to reach Oban. As already mentioned, the 1.35 p.m. runs as a mixed train from Luib to Crianlarich. From Oban the departures are at 6.25 a.m. and 3 p.m., journey times being $8\frac{1}{2}$ and $7\frac{1}{2}$ hr. respectively; the 3 p.m. offers an Assured Arrival Service. Some fish traffic originates at Oban and normally is of sufficiently small proportions to be conveyed by passenger train, but occasionally special trains are run; empty fish vans are returned to Oban by freight train.

Freight trains on the two branch lines consist of one service in each direction. Between passenger duties the Killin branch locomotive leaves Killin with freight traffic to be added to

## OBAN LINE
## LOCOMOTIVES
## OF THE PAST

★The 'Oban bogie' 4-4-0s, built b[...]
Dubs of Glasgow, were special[...]
designed for the Oban line with 5 f[...]
2 in. driving wheels and four-whe[...]
tenders (to limit their length to th[...]
route's small turntables). The first [...]
them appeared in 1882.

★No. 59 was one of the McIntosh '55' Class 4-6-0s built between 1902 and 1905, with 5 ft driving wheels, to replace the 'Oban bogies'. These 4-6-0s were in command of the Oban line for some 20 years.

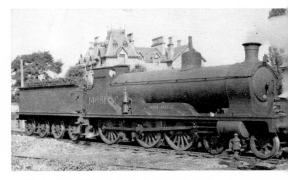

★Pickersgill designed an outside-cylinder 4-6-0 with 5 ft 6 in. driving wheels for the Oban line, which was built by the North British Locomotive Co. in 1922. No. 14623 is seen at Glasgow in L.M.S. days.
[J. C. White

★After the 1923 grouping ex-Highland Railway 'Castle' Class 4-6-0s, like No. 14681 *Skibo Castle*, occasionally ventured on to the Oban line.

★In the 1930s a number of former Highland Railway 'Clan' 4-6-0s were sent to the Oban line and were its mainstay until the arrival of the Stanier Class '5s'. Illustrated is No. 14769 *Clan Cameron*.

[H. C. Casserley

the 6.25 a.m. from Oban and returns at 9.20 a.m. with traffic off the 6.15 a.m. from Stirling. In addition there are two mixed trains each way at 10.3 a.m. and 1.42 p.m. from Killin and 8.12 a.m. and 7.40 p.m. from Killin Junction. The Ballachulish branch has a separate locomotive for its freight traffic, leaving Oban at 3.30 a.m. and reaching Ballachulish at 6.55 a.m. After shunting in the yard here it returns on weekdays at 1.5 p.m., connecting at Connel Ferry with the 3 p.m. from Oban.

As with many L.M.S. routes previously worked by a variety of pre-grouping classes, the Oban line was one of the first to be handed over to the Stanier Class '5' 4-6-0s. From 1937 onwards the number in use steadily increased and so successful were the newcomers that the long-established practice of engine-changing at Stirling was abandoned and new diagrams introduced through workings between Glasgow and Oban. In 1950 a number of Class '5s' were transferred to Stirling and most of the duties on the line were transferred to that depot. Oban depot itself has never had any of these 4-6-0s permanently allocated to it and the actual locomotives used varied considerably, as the large studs at Glasgow and Stirling had diagrams including the Oban line duties. Since the war, ex-L.N.E.R. Class 'B1' and standard Class '5' 4-6-0s have also operated on the Oban line.

Ex-Caledonian 0-6-0s are in regular use on the Ballachulish branch freight and occasionally deputize on the Killin branch duty. For many years passenger services on both the Ballachulish and Killin branches have been handled by ex-Caledonian 0-4-4Ts. The Killin locomotive is sub-shedded at Loch Tay. One of the two engines used on the Ballachulish service remained overnight at the small shed at Ballachulish and after working the first train to Oban was coaled and serviced there before acting as station pilot until its return on the afternoon train. The other locomotive was based at Oban and worked the morning train from Oban, the return trip to Connel Ferry and the afternoon service back.

Now the supremacy of the Class '5' 4-6-0 has been shattered. Diesel-electric locomotives have appeared – at first the N.B. Loco. Co. Type 1,000-h.p. Type 2s, then the Birmingham R.C.W. Co., Sulzer-engined, 1,250-h.p. Type 2s, in each case working in pairs. In the spring of 1962 the latter made almost a clean sweep of the Oban line passenger and freight services;

Class '5s' are now employed to Oban only on special cattle and sheep trains. The diesels are based on Eastfield depot and their Oban duties are part of complex cyclic diagrams which also cover Grangemouth and Edinburgh Princes Street workings and some Glasgow–Stirling local trains. They are too heavy for the Ballachulish branch, whose passenger trains were being handled by Class '2' 2-6-0s Nos. 46468 and 78052 and freight by Class '3F' 0-6-0 No. 57587. The Killin branch 0-4-4T was replaced by Class '4' 2-6-4T No. 80062. Two ex-Caledonian 0-4-4Ts, Nos. 55204/60, were still finding local employment at Oban in mid-April, however.

Oban motive power depot is a small, two-road, timber structure long enough to accommodate two Class '5' 4-6-0s on each road. Beyond it there is a small mechanical coaler. Oban has no large locomotives on its allocation, which consists only of a few engines for the Ballachulish branch freight. The distance of Oban from the nearest large shed necessitates the maintenance of spare locomotives for these duties. Although they have no large locomotives of their own, Oban men handle trains as far east as Crianlarich or Glenoglehead.

Oban station, besides being the terminus of the C.O.R. line, is also the exchange point for travellers to some of the Western Isles, for the mail boats of David MacBrayne tie up alongside the station.

The regular all-year service consists of a daily boat to Tobermory calling at wayside piers on either side of the Sound of Mull, a thrice-weekly mailboat to Tobermory, Coll, Tiree, Castlebay (Barra) and Lochboisdale (S. Uist), and two daily trips to Lismore (3 on Wednesdays). During the summer timetable these are augmented by a daily trip to Staffa and Iona, and a 4-days a week service to Fort William, these being mainly for the benefit of tourists: there are also additional services to Mull and Lismore, and occasional excursion sailings.

The Oban line's traffic is heavy by the standards of Scotland's west coast, but in the present climate of economy this may not be enough to preserve it for the future. In case it should not qualify for Government subsidy under the provisions of the new Railways Bill, it is specially worth a visit – or a succession of visits – lest there should one day be no more opportunities to enjoy its rich scenic beauties.

# Oil by rail from North Thames-side

## By B. PERREN

★Brush Type '2' diesel-electric No. D5508 on L.T.S. Line passenger duty; it is approaching Westcliff with the 11.20 a.m. Fenchurch Street–Shoeburyness in July, 1960.

● Oil in block trainloads figures in the London Tilbury Line's thriving freight; and the working is expedited by enterprising motive power arrangements

IN a review of the London, Tilbury and Southend Line in the 1961 *Trains Illustrated Annual*, I referred briefly to the large volume of petroleum products moving in owners' tank wagons from the oil installations on North Thameside. Since then some very interesting developments in the working of this expanding traffic have been arranged. In 1961 the L.T.S. moved from North Thameside 950,000 tons of petroleum products in owners' tanks – an increase of over 100 per cent on the results three years previously. The sources of this traffic are the large oil storage installation at Thames Haven, the Shell oil refinery at Shell Haven and Mobil's refinery at Coryton, all grouped together on the north side of the Thames; and – to a lesser extent – the two installations at Purfleet operated by Esso and Shell Mex and B.P.

Most of the large oil companies are now taking advantage of rail transport to distribute products from their large marine terminals to inland distribution depots in block train loads, thereby obtaining good utilization of their wagons, favourable rates and transit times, plus the flexibility of loading between various products which is possible with a train of 30 or so tanks. The railway, too, benefits from these arrangements, since regular train loads make possible the preparation of suitable paths and the economic diagramming of train crews and motive power. On the L.T.S., all block trainloads originate from Thames Haven.

Originally a passenger line, with an intermediate station at Mucking, the $3\frac{3}{4}$-mile Thames Haven branch leaves the Pitsea–Tilbury section of the Tilbury loop at Thames Haven Junction, between Stanford-Le-Hope and Low Street, facing the Tilbury direction. There are no passing loops between the branch junction and Thames Haven; the branch is controlled by a single-line token system between Thames Haven Junction and a small frame located outside the Thames Haven Yardmaster's office. At the end of the branch there are several marshalling sidings where the trains are formed by L.T.S. staff for departure; loaded outgoing or empty incoming tanks are shunted between this yard and the various private sidings by a B.R. 350 h.p. diesel shunter. Mobil's Coryton refinery is just over a mile from Thames Haven and is reached by a section of the Corringham Light Railway, now acquired by the company for the transfer of their tank car traffic from Coryton to the L.T.& S. at Thames Haven.

Each weekday some 14 oil trains leave Thames Haven for various destinations; of this total, 10 trains run regularly to the private sidings serving oil company distribution depots. Full details of the departures are shown in the table. In addition to the through block trains, there is a regular forwarding by the oil companies of individual tank wagons to various destinations on B.R. To cater for this traffic, three trains run each day from Thames Haven to the

L.T.&S. yard at Ripple Lane for shunting and transfer there to the ordinary merchandise trains of general North Thameside traffic; transfers for L.M.R. destinations are conveyed by a fourth service at 1.30 p.m. to Brent. The remaining trains in the table are all block loads.

Except for the 6.45 p.m. to Neasden, only required to run on two days each week with one set of tanks, the pattern for the remaining block trains is that each is operated by two sets of tank cars in circuit between Thames Haven and the destination. One set of tanks is loaded on the sidings at Thames Haven during the day, whilst the second set is unloaded at the inland terminal; during the night B.R. work out the loaded train and return the previous day's tanks for re-loading. This system of operation has enabled good train working arrangements, particularly in the utilization of the 18 Brush Type '2' 1,250 or 1,365 h.p. diesels now covering almost all of the L.T.&S. freight workings. The few remaining steam duties are soon to be replaced by diesels. In steam days, apart from a few cross-London transfer trips, it was usual for L.T.&S. crews to work mainly over their own home territory; but today, with the necessity to achieve the highest possible utilization of the new motive power

## DAILY L.T.S OIL TRAIN DEPARTURES

| Depart | Destination | Route | Loading | Motive Power |
|---|---|---|---|---|
| 3.15 a.m. | Royston (E.R.) | Canonbury, G.N. main line† | Block for S.M.&B.P. | Tilbury: a 2-8-0 throughout |
| 9.33 a.m. | Rowley Regis (W.R.) | Acton, Didcot, Oxford, Worcester | Block for S.M. & B.P. | L.T.S. diesel to Didcot |
| 12.5 p.m. | Ripple Lane | Direct | Misc. transfer | Brush diesel |
| 1.30 p.m. | Brent (L.M.R.) | † | L.M.R. transfers | Brush diesel |
| 4.25 p.m. | Ripple Lane | Direct | Misc. transfers | Brush diesel |
| 5.45 p.m. | Ripple Lane | Direct | Misc. transfers | Brush diesel |
| 6.20 p.m. | Rugby | L.M. main line via Northampton* | Block for Mobil/Charrington to Coventry | L.T.S. diesel to Rugby |
| 6.45 p.m. | Neasden | Cricklewood† | Block Esso load for L.T.E. | L.M.R. power |
| 9 p.m. | Hethersett (E.R.) | Stratford, Cambridge | Block Esso load | L.T.S. diesel to Cambridge |
| 9.25 p.m. | Thame (W.R.) | Acton, High Wycombe* | S.M.&B.P. block | L.T.S. diesel to Acton |
| 9.58 p.m. | Langley Green (W.R.) | Acton, Banbury* | S.M.&B.P. block | L.T.S. diesel to Acton |
| 5.5 p.m. | Royston (E.R.) | Canonbury, G.N. main line† | S.M.&B.P. block | L.T.S. diesel to Finsbury Park |
| 11 p.m. | Rowley Regis | Acton, Didcot* Oxford, Worcester | S.M.&B.P. block | L.T.S. diesel to Didcot |
| 11.30 p.m. | Northampton | L.M. Main Line* | S.M.&B.P. block | L.M.R. power |

**Routes from L.T.S.:**    * Barking, South Tottenham, Gospel Oak, Willesden.
                          † Barking, Forest Gate, Stratford, Victoria Park.

and the opportunity afforded by the new oil train developments, L.T.&S. crews are working well beyond the confines of the Line to destinations as far as Cambridge on G.E. territory Didcot on the W.R. and Rugby on the L.M.R.

In steam days there were three motive power depots on the L.T.&S. – Shoeburyness, Tilbury and Plaistow. At the time of writing, when electric trains are taking over steam passenger workings as new stock is available, the depot arrangements are in a transitionary stage. Shoeburyness is still in operation as the main steam depot, but will ultimately become an electric depot; Tilbury is still open but will ultimately become a signing-on point; and Plaistow is now used as a stabling point for steam engines between the peak passenger services. A new motive power depot for diesel locomotives has been opened at Ripple Lane, adjoining the new yard; enginemen have been transferred there from Plaistow and Tilbury for freight work. Crews for the new electric services will be based on the new East Ham electric depot or will sign on at Tilbury. The longer distance L.T.S. freight turns are all covered from Ripple Lane. Ripple Lane's allocation of 18 Brush diesels actually is part of the G.E. line's Stratford allocation. The diesels receive more detailed maintenance at Stratford, but while working the L.T.&S. cyclic diagrams each locomotive has a daily pit examination at Ripple Lane.

The current oil train schedules have been developed gradually over the past three or four years to the present pattern as new traffic has been obtained, more diesel locomotives have been delivered, and when opportunities to improve the workings with other Regions have arisen. An example of this is the working to Rugby described later. Two trains, the 6.45 p.m. Neasden and the 11.30 p.m. Northampton, are worked by the L.M.R. – the first by a Neasden steam engine, the latter by two Devons Road English Electric Type '1s' in multiple.

L.T.S. men work over the Tottenham & Hampstead line with the 9.25 p.m. Thame and 9.58 p.m. Langley Green trains as far as Acton where they hand over their trains to the W.R. for the rest of the journey. It has been possible to arrange the times of the trains so that the returning empty tanks from Thame and Langley Green form the return working from Acton.

Esso's nightly train to Hethersett, on the G.E. line between Ely and Norwich, is a more recent development and shortly after it was in-

troduced Ripple Lane men began working it to Cambridge. At Cambridge the L.T.&S. diesel comes off and changes places with an English Electric Type '4' on the empty returning tanks from Hethersett. Two trains run each day to S.M.&B.P's depot at Royston, on the G.N. Hitchin–Cambridge branch. The 5.5 p.m. Royston is worked through by a Brush diesel to Clarence Yard, on the G.N. Line, where it comes off the train to work back returning empties from Royston, which are taken over at the G.N. Line's Ferme Park yard. A G.N. Brush diesel completes the Royston working. The second Royston train at 3.15 a.m. is still steam-powered by a 'WD' 2-8-0 from Tilbury depot, working throughout. Tilbury men work to Clarence Yard, changing footplates there to join the returning 'WD' 2-8-0-hauled empties. This turn was to be dieselized during 1962.

A new requirement of S.M.&B.P. for a train of products from Thames Haven to Rowley Regis was planned from the outset on the basis of haulage through to Didcot by Ripple Lane locomotives and men. This, of course, required L.T.&S. crews to learn a considerable section of new route - the 50 miles from Acton to Didcot. Didcot was selected as the exchange point, since this is the practical limitation of a round trip from Ripple Lane within a driver's normal day. On each of the two trains now running separate crews cover the section between Thames Haven and Ripple Lane. Both Rowley Regis trains are Class 'F' and load up to 29 vehicles.

Early in 1959, a new regular haul was instituted of Mobil supplies from Coryton to their depot at Tile Hill, near Coventry, which is served by a private siding on the L.M.R. Rugby–Birmingham main line. To work the service the firm built 44 power-braked tank cars, each carrying 5,900 gal. of gas oil, diesel or a light petroleum distillate for the West Midlands Gas Board. Initially the train only ran on two days per week, but this was soon extended to a daily working. Two sets of tanks are in circuit between Thames Haven and Coventry; they are loaded at Coryton and worked by Mobil's own diesel shunter to Thames Haven. Mobil's associates, Charringtons, also have a depot in the Coventry area at Hawkesbury Lane, which is supplied from Thames Haven, and this traffic has been combined with the Tile Hill train.

Until September, 1961, the L.T.&S. worked the combined Tile Hill and Hawkesbury Lane train as far as Willesden, where the formation was divided and worked forward as two separate trains by L.M.R. Class '5' 4-6-0s. The L.T.&S. diesel and trainmen returned from Willesden to Thames Haven with the combined empty tanks off the previous night's outward load. following discussions between the L.T.&S. and the L.M.R. Western Lines, it was agreed that L.T.&S. diesels and men would work the combined load out as far as Rugby, handing the train over there to the L.M.R. and returning southwards with the empty tanks. This arrangement eliminated a somewhat lengthy layover of the Tilbury crews at Willesden, improved the employment of the Brush diesels used on the train, and saved the L.M.R. a path in each direction over their busy main line between Willesden and Rugby as well as the crews and power to work the trains. Following a successful trial working to Rugby and back early in 1961, Ripple Lane men started to learn the road to Rugby and the new schedules became operative in September, 1961.

Recently, through facilities kindly arranged by the L.T.&S. Line Traffic Manager, I was able to see at first hand the working of the Coventry oil train when I made the journey from Thames Haven to Rugby and back as far as Ripple Lane. The full schedule of the train and forward workings from Rugby to Coventry are shown in the accompanying table. Accompanied by the L.T.&S. Movement Superinten-

dent, we reached Thames Haven about half-an-hour before departure time as the Mobil shunter was transferring the tanks from Coryton into the B.R. sidings. Since the total weight of the train generally exceeds 1,200 gross tons, two Brush diesels in multiple are required for the working. On the night of my journey – in mid-January – two 1,365 h.p. locos had been allocated to the Rugby job, No. D5697 leading D5617; the gangway connections enabling easy passage between the two engines had been made. On the outward journey I travelled in the cab of the leading diesel through to Rugby. To facilitate the division of the train at Rugby and reversal at Tile Hill brake-vans are attached at each end of the Mobil section, plus the usual brake at the rear of the train following the Hawkesbury Lane tanks. From Thames Haven the formation was: brake van; 12 Charringtons tanks; brake van; two low wagons as 'runners'; 20 Mobil tanks; two empty vans as 'runners'; and guard's brake – a gross weight of some 1,229 tons. Here I should mention the purpose of the empty 'runner' wagons between the engine and the loaded tank cars; because of the low flash point of certain types of petroleum products two such wagons are marshalled as a safety measure.

A few minutes before 6.20 p.m. our driver received the 'right away' from the guard and, with a short blast of the locomotive's horn, moved the controller over to the first notch to get the vast load on the move out of the yard. As we passed the yardmaster's office the assistant driver collected the single line token for the section to Thames Haven Junction. The single-line branch runs alongside the floodlit Shell Haven oil refinery, past vast-oil storage tanks and, towards the end of the line, Fison's plant. We were allowed 15 min. to pass Thames Haven Junction, where we slowed to join the main line to Tilbury, now signalled throughout with colour-lights. As far as Ripple Lane the schedule is fairly easy – faster running at that time of the evening is not desirable because of checks from commuter trains. We were slightly checked approaching Tilbury East Junction by the 6.40 p.m. diesel m.u. train from Tilbury Riverside to Pitsea, which crossed our path to gain the loop from Tilbury East to Tilbury West Junctions, although we were not halted. Passing several steam-hauled trains conveying returning city travellers from Fenchurch Street, we made steady progress through the North Thameside industrial scene,

|  | Outward | | Return | |
|---|---|---|---|---|
| THAMES HAVEN . | dep. 6.20 p.m. | | arr. . a.m. | |
| Tilbury East Junction . | pass 6.44 ,, | | pass . ,, | |
| Ripple Lane | arr. 7.20 ,, | | dep. 3.46 ,, | |
| Ripple Lane South | dep. 7.22 ,, | | arr. 3.45 ,, | |
| Tottenham Junction Road | pass 7.50 ,, | | pass 3.20 ,, | |
| Junction . | ,, 7.59 ,, | | ,, 3.10 ,, | |
| Gospel Oak | ,, 8.06 ,, | | ,, 3.04 ,, | |
| WILLESDEN BEST SIDINGS | arr. 8.25 ,, | | dep. 2.46 ,, | |
|  | dep. 8.35 ,, | | arr. 2.44 ,, | |
| Watford . | pass 9.03 ,, | | pass 2.25 ,, | |
| Tring | ,, 9.21 ,, | | ,, 1.55 ,, | |
| Bletchley . | ,, 9.49 ,, | | ,, 1.33 ,, | |
| Roade | ,, 10.09 ,, | | ,, 1.13 ,, | |
| Northampton . | ,, 10.20 ,, | | ,, 1.00 ,, | |
| RUGBY MIDLAND | ,, 10.55 ,, | | dep. 12.30 ,, | |
| HAWKESBURY LANE . | dep. 5.45 a.m. | 7.30 a.m. | arr. 7.28 p.m. | 5.33 p.m. |
|  | arr. 6.16 a.m. | | dep. 6.10 p.m. | |
| TILE HILL . | arr. | 10.07 a.m. | dep. | 4.55 p.m. |

un-checked until Ripple Lane; here we stopped on the main line at a signal near the office block on the yard where Ripple Lane enginemen and guards sign on for duty. The Ripple Lane crew which works through to Rugby took over and I made the acquaintence of Driver Frank Davis and his mate.

A former Plaistow steam driver transferred to the new Ripple Lane depot, Davis had for several years driven Class '4' 2-6-4 tanks on Shoeburyness and Tilbury passenger trains, but was now a member of a link of 12 men working Brush diesels, mainly on freight. Before taking a turn on the new Rugby duty he had, in company with his 11 colleagues, to learn the road from Willesden to Rugby. Involving both fast and slow lines to Roade, the Northampton loop and the Blisworth Northampton line – all new ground to L.T.&S. men – this was no easy task.

Starting away again from Ripple Lane we had clear signals all the way through the new Barking layout and full power was applied to get the load over the main flyover, our route to the Tottenham & Hampstead Line. Due to a slight delay to the 7.23 p.m. Barking–Kentish Town stopping diesel train, we preceeded instead of following this train through to Junction Road and were thus able to get across to Gospel Oak in good time, but ahead of schedule. Unfortunately, the Gospel Oak signalman could not let us have the road through the junction and we were brought to a brief halt.

At the time of my journey the 6.20's schedule allowed a 10 min. stop at Brent Sidings, Willesden, to take on an L.M.R. pilotmen if required by the L.T.&S. crew; but as sufficient L.T.&S. men are now qualified to work to Rugby this is no longer necessary. Since Driver Davis had learned the road to Rugby, we had no need to stop at Willesden and we were fortunate to have a clear road right through the area on to the down relief lines. With the smart run across from Ripple Lane and time saved at Willesden we were now about 25 min. ahead of our booked time. Of course, freight trains do have booked times, which are adhered to, but there is operating flexibility to allow them to run early if the overall traffic position as seen in the district control office makes this desirable. Such were the circumstances on this night. Running steadily down the relief lines well before time, we were checked approaching Watford; this proved to be the Watford distant, which was on as we were to take the

junction north of Watford station to cross on to the down main. We passed Watford at 8.34 with an ample margin in front of the 8.30 p.m. down 'West Coast Postal' from Euston, for which postmen were then attaching mailbags to the apparatus beyond the station.

Apart from a 20 m.p.h. p.w. caution in Kilsby Tunnel there was no other interference with our progress to Rugby. Full power was applied for the remainder of the climb up to Tring summit, whereafter we settled down to a steady 60 m.p.h. – the maximum for a Class 'C' freight – until the slack in Kilsby Tunnel. Beyond the tunnel, we ambled down past Hillmorton towards Rugby, where we turned into the yard at 9.54 p.m., just over an hour early. We had run the 66 miles from Watford to Rugby in the creditable time of 80 min.; however, this was partly the result of running main line and not by way of Northampton.

Before we could carry out the task of shunting the train back from the reception lines into the sidings, appropriately divided into the two sections, we had to await clearance of the north end of the yard by a departing northbound freight. This train did not leave until the down 'Irish Mail' had passed. After shunting operations had been completed, our locomotives moved on to the Birmingham line to reverse back across the layout and collect the return train from the sidings adjoining Rugby No. 1 signalbox. We marshalled the two sections from Tile Hill and Hawkesbury Lane and set about the important task of preparing a welcome supper on the small electric cooker provided in the locomotive's engine compartment.

Our southbound departure was some 12 min. behind time at 12.42 and we were signalled out on to the up Northampton line. At Roade the two lines from Northampton join the main lines from Rugby through Kilsby Tunnel and become the relief lines through to Willesden. As on the down journey, the normal path for the return train to Thames Haven is on the relief line. We were still late passing Roade, but at Wolverton were turned on to the up main line, where we remained until Sudbury Junction, Wembley. This enabled us to recover the lost minutes and pass Willesden practically on time. Apart from one or two adverse distant signals on the electrified lines from Willesden Junction through to Gospel Oak, which cleared as we approached them, we were unchecked until we reached Junction

★Two Brush Type '2' diesels negotiate the Tilbury triangle with the Thames Haven- Tile Hill and Hawkesbury Lane oil train from the L.T.S. Line to the L.M.R.
[*British Railways*

Road. Here we stopped for 10 min. This delay was due to checks from two cross-London transfer freights en route to Temple Mills and Ripple Lane, which we had to follow to South Tottenham. With several more checks further time was lost and Ripple Lane was reached 29 min. late at 4.14 a.m.

Thus concluded, for me, a most instructive journey, packed throughout with railway interest. Despite the late return arrival, I still remain convinced that in the field of long distance bulk haulage British Railways have no serious rivals for fast, cheap and reliable movement of freight traffic.

## EARLY DAYS WITH THE 'A4s'

(*Concluded from page* 12)
*Lancer* with Samwells, No. 4475 *Flying Fox* with Holland, and so on. This practice of giving each man his own engine had been established at Kings Cross, as at most other depots, for very many years – since the old Great Northern days, in fact. There were few more heinous crimes than to book a driver's regular engine to someone else.

Because of the fair proportion of lodging turns worked by the top links it was not difficult to adhere to this principle; men and engines travelled down to York, Leeds or Newcastle one day and returned together the next. The policy had its risks, however. It could lead to the dubious practice of deliberately booking to fast, heavy and important main-line expresses engines that were known to be past their best

or in a generally run-down condition, simply because these were the engines of specific crews rostered to the turns. Meanwhile, the cream of the depot stock might be running only on short-distance, relatively light and unimportant trains. Up to a point, knowledge of his engine's condition and its capabilities and foibles, together with his intention and ability to get the very best out of it, enabled a driver to put up a satisfactory performance; but perhaps these were not the best means by which to attain that end.

With the first of the 'A4s' came the opportunity to break down the tradition of giving each top link driver his own engine. In working the 'Silver Jubilee' it was impossible to keep men and engines together; at first there were simply not enough streamlined Pacifics for every man to have his own, and consequently each set of enginemen, as they came round to the turn, had to take out the same one, No. 2509, or later on, one of Nos. 2511 and 2512. Nobody seemed particularly to notice this change at the time, perhaps because of the excitement of running the streamliners, and no very strong protests were made. The thin end of the wedge had been safely inserted.

For the same reason, a similar arrangement had to be adopted in the case of the other two high-speed trains, the 'Coronation' and 'West Riding Limited'. In the summer of 1937, all boats were burned, and thenceforward a specific locomotive was assigned to the only train that ever really mattered to me – the Edinburgh 'non-stop'.

MEMBERS OF THE
PUBLIC MUST NOT
PASS BEYOND
THIS NOTICE

**Left:** Class 'A1' 4-6-2 No. 60130 *Kestrel* prepares to leave Kings Cross with the 10.25 a.m. express to Leeds on a December Sunday in 1960.
[*P. H. Wells*

# EAST
# COAST
# PACIFICS

**Below:** The up 'White Rose' passes Beeston Junction, soon after leaving Leeds for Kings Cross behind Class 'A3' 4-6-2 No. 60070 *Gladiateur*.
[*Eric Treacy*

★English Electric Type '4' 2,000 h.p. diesel-electric No. D209 threads Hadley Wood with the 12.20 p.m. Hull–Kings Cross express in April, 1960.  [C. P. Boocock

# In the cab of an English Electric type '4'

## by P. RANSOME-WALLIS

**● The East Coast main line seen from the driver's desk of a diesel.**

ONE of the brighter aspects of the dieselization programme of British Railways has been some of the work done on the East Coast main line by English Electric Type '4' 1Co-Co1 diesel-electric locomotives. Observation of the express services on this line at points north of Hitchin (where the line to Cambridge diverges) reveals a uniformity of diesel motive power – the 'Deltics' apart – which is almost unique in Britain, where politics and too-free enterprise have so far bedevilled all efforts at standardization of equipment. Furthermore, in these Type '4' locomotives the Operating department has found a reasonably reliable machine which has become well liked by both the locomotive men and the maintenance staffs.

The prime mover is a medium-speed four-cycle, 16-cylinder supercharged V-type diesel engine, developing 675 h.p. at 450 r.p.m. and 2,000 h.p. at 850 r.p.m.; the engine speed is continuously variable between these limits. The engine is direct-coupled to a d.c. generator of the 10-pole self-ventilating type, which at 850 r.p.m. has a continuous rating of 1,320 kw., 1,800 amps, 730 volts; a direct-coupled auxiliary generator has a continuous rating of 48 kw., 436 amps, 110 volts, at the same speed. Six force-ventilated traction motors are axle-hung and nose-suspended; each has a continuous rating of 212 h.p., 600 amps., 300 volts, or a one-hour rating of 650 amps, 300 volts. The six traction motors are grouped in pairs, each pair being in parallel, but the two motors of each pair are in series. The motor control incorporates three stages of field weakening over which the driver has no control. These conditions are introduced and withdrawn automatically according to the voltage and amperage of the motors as determined by the load regulator control. The introduction of field weakening is critical and occurs when the voltage across the traction motors reaches 350 volts.

Driving the Type '4' is simple, easy and as near foolproof as is possible. Riding in the cab of No. D242 of Gateshead shed on the 11 a.m. Kings Cross–Edinburgh express in mid-1961, I realized to the full what a comfortable job diesel railroading had become. The driver has a well-upholstered seat behind a large glass windscreen and screen-wipers and screen-

is started by depressing the appropriate button, whereafter power is re-applied.

The cab is quiet in running and is snug, warm and free from draughts – on the warm and sunny March day of my journey, in fact, it was too warm. The Type '4s' ride exceptionally well, although the provision of a leading guide wheel in each bogie is now not regarded as modern practice and was incorporated in this design to reduce the maximum axle-loading at the Civil Engineer's request. On my journey, the fireman made some excellent black coffee on the electric cooking stove and a full cup placed on the control panel never spilled a drop.

I rode with No. D242 as far as York. As can be seen by the accompanying table, the diesel had plenty in hand all the way and timekeeping was essentially a matter of holding back so as not to get too far ahead of schedule. At the time of my trip, it should be noted, there were 22 min. of recovery time in the 213 min. schedule for the 188 miles from Kings Cross to York.

★Camera in the cab of an English Electric Type '4' on the East Coast route – (**above**) looking ahead near Naburn as Class 'V2' 2-6-2 No. 60852 approaches on an up fitted freight; and (**right**) focused on the driver, with his hand on the controller in the right foreground, as No. D242 rolls at 80 m.p.h.

washers take away most of the hazards of bad weather, while the Automatic Warning System provides all possible aid in fog. True, the dead-man's pedal must be kept depressed while running, but apart from this the infinitely variable electro-pneumatic controller (the main power handle) and the brake valve handle are the only essential controls, once the engine has been started and the reverser handle is correctly positioned.

To start the train, the main power handle is moved gently backwards from the 'off' position towards the 'full power' position until the main ammeter shows a reading. It is then gradually advanced until the requisite power has been obtained. When the locomotive is accelerating, however, the current must never be allowed to exceed 2,600 amps. Should there be any wheel slip, an amber light above the control panel is illuminated and the power is automatically reduced. If this is not adequate to prevent further slipping, the driver returns the main power handle to the 'off' position and sanding

### KING'S CROSS—YORK

| Miles | Location | Schedule | Actual | Speed | Controller | Current |
|---|---|---|---|---|---|---|
| | | min. | min. sec. | m.p.h. | | amps. |
| 0.0 | KINGS CROSS . | 0 | 0 : 0 | — | off | 1,700 |
| 2.50 | Finsbury Park . | [2] | 5 : 10 | 38 | full | 1,700 |
| 12.70 | Potters Bar . | 20 | 19 : 30 | 58 | full | 1,900 |
| 17.70 | Hatfield . . | 25 | 24 : 40 | 60 | full | |
| | Welwyn G. C. . | p.w.s. | | 20 | | |
| | Stevenage . | p.w.s. | | 15 | | |
| 31.90 | Hitchin . . | 39 | 40 : 05 | 76 | full | 1,400 |
| 44.15 | Sandy . . | 48 | 48 : 30 | 78 | | |
| | | [4] | | | | |
| 58.85 | Huntingdon . | 64 5 | 59 : 50 | 70/80 | full | 1,600 |
| 76.35 | PETERBOROUGH arr. . | 86 | 76 : 50 | — | off | — |
| 0.0 | dep. . . | 0 | 0 : 0 | — | — | |
| 3.15 | Werrington Jnc. . | 7 | 6 : 45 | 62 | full | 1,100 |
| 12.30 | Essendine . | 16 | 14 : 00 | 69 | full | 1,200 |
| | | p.w.s. | | 18 | | |
| 20.75 | Corby Glen . | [5] | | 58 | full | 1,650 |
| 23.75 | Stoke Box . | 32 | 28 : 05 | 58 | full | 1,900 |
| 29.10 | Grantham . | 37 | 32 : 10 | 70 | | |
| 33.35 | Barkston . | 41 | 35 : 45 | 76 | | |
| 43.75 | Newark . | 49 | 44 : 00 | 74 | | |
| | | sigs. | | 52 | | |
| 62.25 | Retford . | 69 | 61 : 30 | 58 | | |
| | Scrooby . | p.w.s. | | 15 | | |
| | Loversall Carr . | p.w.s. | | 20 | | |
| | Black Carr Jnc. . | p.w.s. | | 20 | | |
| | | [4] | | | | |
| 79.60 | Doncaster . | 90 [2] | 86 : 00 | 50 | full | 1,510 |
| 83.85 | Shaftholme Jnc. . | 97 | 90 : 40 | 74 | full | 1,400 |
| | | sigs. | | 40 | | |
| 97.95 | Selby . . | 110 | 105 : 00 | 40 | full | 1,600 |
| 111.80 | YORK . . | 127 | 119 : 30 | — | off | |

This proved an over-generous allowance and became more of an embarrassment than a blessing.

The maximum load for these locomotives is determined by the schedule to be operated. Generally, the overall performance of the Type '4' is considered to be equal to that of the average performance of an East Coast Pacific. However, with good coal and in good mechanical condition, an expertly handled 'A1' or 'A4' Pacific is capable of a much superior performance, except perhaps in initial acceleration.

Undoubtedly the greatest attribute of these and other diesel-electric locomotives is their ability to accelerate rapidly. I thought it would be a very good Pacific which could accelerate a 348-ton train from 18 m.p.h. at Little Bytham to 58 m.p.h. at Stoke summit, as did No. D242. In addition, the diesels are capable of working efficiently all types of trains; they are thus true mixed traffic machines and a more flexible tool to the operator's hand.

My impression of No. D242 at high speed was rather disappointing. One got the feeling that the locomotive was incapable of achieving its rated maximum of 90 m.p.h., though I am aware that such high speed has frequently been achieved with these locomotives. A very great proportion of the running was made with the main power handle fully open, yet nowhere did speed exceed 80 m.p.h. and it was usually no more than 74–76 m.p.h. on the level with 'nothing more to come'. After the splendid liveliness of the Pacifics at high speeds, one could not avoid a feeling of frustration.

Of steam-heating boilers there is scarcely any good to be said by anybody. They are far and away the greatest cause of failure on the Type '4', as on all other diesels. The boilers are oil-fired and their water tanks can be replenished from track troughs by means of an air-operated water scoop which can fill the tanks in 30 seconds at 60 m.p.h. The scoop is lowered vertically and has two up-takes so that water can be scooped with the locomotive running in either direction. After a very shaky start, the boiler on D242 gave up the ghost at Retford and had to be shut down. Fortunately the warm weather proved sufficient for the passengers without extra heat. At present there seems to be no satisfactory answer to the boiler problem in this country. Among the enginemen, the general opinion is that the boilers would work splendidly if heating a building, but that the vibration of a locomotive is too much for a number of their details, as failures occur from many causes. Personally, I think there is much to be said for a separate boiler wagon carrying an oil-fired locomotive type boiler with a feed water pump, although one is also aware of the disadvantages.

The maintenance of the Type '4' locomotives is carried out at running sheds and consists of two examination schedules – one mechanical and one electrical; the latter covers not only generators and traction motors but also such details as light bulbs and the breakfast cooker. The maintenance schedules vary a little as between one Region and another. Both examination schedules are carried out on a time basis and not on the completion of specified mileage. They are under continuous review in order to try to get more mileage between examinations. At the time of writing there are daily, weekly, monthly, three-monthly and six-monthly examinations of electrical and mechanical components. The daily examinations include a complete visual examination of the locomotive by both mechanical and electrical maintenance staff every day, or part of a day, in which the locomotive is in service, 'to detect loose, missing or defective parts.' Fuel oil, lubricating oil, water, and all fire-fighting equipment are among items checked daily and replenished as necessary. Weekly and monthly examinations involve more detailed and searching checks including, for example, the monthly removal of the engine crankcase doors to check lubrication of main, big end and small end bearings, and the cleaning of brush gear and insulators of all electrical machines. The three- and six-monthly examinations cover the entire mechanical and electrical parts of the locomotive.

The English Electric Type '4' is guaranteed by the manufacturer for twelve months against faulty material and workmanship and any serious failure is dealt with at the builder's works. In the case of failure of small components, the necessary item is sent to the running shed concerned where it is replaced, often under the supervision of English Electric engineers.

It is at present the policy that all except the most trivial repairs are dealt with either by the manufacturer or by B.R. main works. This was undoubtedly sound practice with new and 'temperamental' locomotives, but as time goes on the running sheds may justifiably expect to be entrusted with more major repairs, especially as many have new and well-equipped diesel maintenance shops. One reason for the centralization of repairs is probably the shortage of spare parts. This is an unsatisfactory state of affairs as it often means keeping a locomotive out of traffic perhaps for several days, in order to obtain some comparatively small item.

The scarcity of skilled men, especially electricians, is also apt to slow up maintenance schedules at the sheds, but most places to which the Type '4' is allocated have recruited a hard core of skilled men – some electricians come from generator stations – and others are being trained. The shortage of diesel-trained footplate staff is also a problem which will gradually be solved, but with the general shortage of enginemen throughout the country, training programmes give rise to some severe headaches for shedmasters!

Such problems of maintenance and manning greatly affect the present locomotive availability and most depots confidently expect significant increases in monthly mileage per locomotive in the future. The present mileage for the Type '4' on the East Coast is, however, by no means unsatisfactory and No. D201, for example, completed 400,000 miles in its first three years' service, some of which was spent in crew-training.

With the exception of the steam heating boiler, the English Electric Type '4s' are running with virtually no mechanical troubles and failures are few and from varied causes. Earlier failures caused by such things as blown fuses or the unintentional opening of a circuit breaker now present few difficulties and can be put right immediately as the enginemen become more experienced and confident. An undoubted step forward is the fact that suitable hand tools have been issued to diesel locomotive enginemen to enable them to effect simple running repairs on the road.

The success of diesel traction on British Railways depends on the elimination of a very large proportion of the present expensive and heterogeneous collection of diesel locomotives and the standardization of five or six suitably powered units. The present muddle is deplored by railwaymen at all levels and probably the small boy with his train-spotting manual is the only one who is pleased. The success of the Type '4s' is therefore a welcome step in the right direction.

---

**Facing page:**

## KENTISH CAMEOS OF YESTERDAY

★With both Phase I and Phase II of the Southern Region's Kent Coast main line electrification completed, steam scenes such as these have become history. The pictures show: **(top)** a Maidstone–Dover stopping train, hauled by Class '4' 2-6-4T No. 80065, passing a Minster–Shorncliffe stopping train, hauled by Class 'N' 2-6-0 No. 31407, in Folkestone Warren in April, 1960; **(centre)** a 'Battle of Britain' Class Pacific at the head of a Victoria–Dover boat train overtaking the now withdrawn Class 'D1' 4-4-0 No. 31749 on an excursion at Bromley South in June, 1957; and **(bottom)** 'Schools' 4-4-0 No. 30921 *Shrewsbury* passing through Folkestone Warren with a relief Dover–Victoria boat train in April, 1960.

[*M. R. Galley (centre)*,
*D. Cross*

★'King' 4-6-0 No. 6016 *King Edward V* storms Dainton bank with the 9.30 a.m. Paddington–Plymouth in February, 1959.

[D. S. Fish

# Fifty years of steam between Paddington and Plymouth

## By CECIL J. ALLEN

**● A tribute to the engines and men who set high standards on the West of England main line before diesels.**

WITH the virtual disappearance of steam from the passenger services between Paddington and the West of England, the time is ripe for a review of the work of Great Western locomotives during their long reign over this important route. It was not until the succession in 1902 of George Jackson Churchward to the position of Chief Mechanical Engineer at Swindon that G.W.R. locomotive work really began to come into the limelight; but in the very next year, 1903, one of his engines had achieved the first of a series of outstanding feats that were destined to make his name famous in the locomotive world.

The hand of Churchward in Swindon locomotive design had become plainly evident well before the resignation of his previous chief, William Dean. It was seen in various changes that were quite new to British eyes, such as the saddle-supported extended smokebox, the high Belpaire firebox, in the front corners of which a perforated pipe collected the steam, and the boiler barrel crowned by a safety-valve column; with these were combined double frames, with the coupling rods working on outside cranks, and bogies with outside bearings. Various Dean 4-4-os had given a preview of these changes before the first all-Churchward express passenger design, the 'City' class 4-4-os, emerged from Swindon Works in 1903. These embodied other principles which were to make Churchward's engines amongst the freest-running at speed of any in the country, in particular a long valve-travel, large exhaust ports and a high working pressure; also for the first time they were fitted with taper boilers. With the 'Cities', Churchward was for a time content with a pressure of 195 lb per sq in., but very soon he was moving forward to the 225 lb which became standard with all his later express engines.

In the year of its completion, the first 'City', No. 3433 *City of Bath*, put up an astonishing performance on an occasion which surely can have no parallel in British railway history. The Prince and Princess of Wales – later King George V and Queen Mary – were making a journey to fulfil some engagements in the West Country and it was therefore decided to accommodate themselves and their party in two saloons attached to an advance portion of the 10.40 a.m. down Penzance express. This was three years before the opening of the direct Westbury route and though the 3 p.m. from Paddington at that time ran non-stop daily over the 193.6 miles to Exeter via Bristol. the 10.40 a.m. normally halted at both Bristol and Exeter. But on this occasion it was decided to work the five-coach special non-stop over the entire 245.6 miles from Paddington to North Road, Plymouth; and the engine selected to haul the 130-ton train was *City of Bath*, in the charge of Driver Burden.

All that is known about the preparations for the journey is that it had been intimated to the G.W.R. authorities that the royal party would like to have 'a good run'. But when we remember the scrupulous care with which royal specials are normally worked, with passing times laid down at every station *en route*, it seems almost unbelievable that the said 'good run' of July 14, 1903 should have brought the royal train into Plymouth no less than 37 min. ahead of schedule; yet so it was. By Old Oak Common *City of Bath* was doing 60 m.p.h., by West Drayton 70 and through Didcot 77; as far as Bathampton, where speed was reduced for the Bath curve, it never fell below 70 m.p.h. for 91 miles continuously, and at the foot of Dauntsey bank 87½ m.p.h. was attained. Swindon, 77.3 miles, was passed in 68 min. 1 sec.; Bath, 106.85 miles, in 92 min. 2 sec.; and, after a very cautious negotiation of the Bristol avoiding line, Pylle Hill Junction, 118.4 miles, in 104 min. 42 sec. – an improvement on the 'Bristolian' 105-min. schedule to Temple Meads introduced thirty-two years later.

Then came a resumption of the high speed; at Yatton 77 m.p.h. was reached once again and speed remained in the seventies until a slight reduction for Taunton (162.8 miles in 142 min.

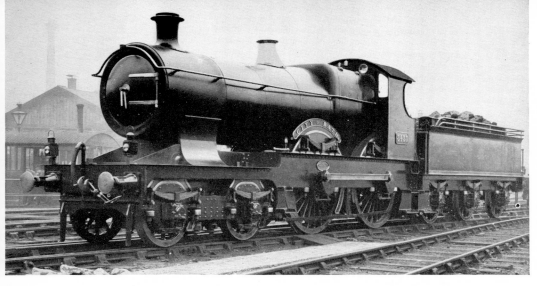

39 sec.), after which *City of Bath* charged up Wellington bank to achieve a minimum of 50 m.p.h. over Whiteball Summit. Despite easy running over the winding track in the Culm valley, while the royal party was at lunch, Exeter was passed in 172 min. 34 sec. – a distance of 193.6 miles from Paddington via Bristol – and Newton Abbot, 213.8 miles, in 193 min. 51 sec. The gruelling climb to Dainton Summit was completed at 30 m.p.h. and the 1 in 50 of Rattery bank at 36 m.p.h.; with all the needed caution over the many sharp curves of this final stretch, Burden brought his train to rest in North Road station in 3 hours 53 min. 35 sec. from London, causing no small consternation to the civic authorities in Plymouth, it may be added, by this unexpected disturbance of their reception arrangements! This was indeed a wonderful achievement for a 54½-ton 4-4-0 with 18 in. × 26 in. cylinders and no more than 20.6 sq ft of firegrate.

In the following year, 1904, the 'Cities' were to acquire even more lustre. During 1903 and 1904 eastbound transatlantic liners had begun to make calls at Plymouth and this had initiated a competition between the two rival railways as to which could reach London first, the London & South Western with the passengers and the Great Western with the mails. The G.W.R. had the longer route to cover but the motive power which Churchward had put in its hands was easily superior to that of the other competitor. The zenith of Great Western achievement was reached on May 9, 1904, and once again a 'City' was involved – No. 3440 *City of Truro*. With a five-van mail train of 148 gross tons, Driver Clements achieved the extraordinary feat of maintaining an average of 40.2 m.p.h. up the

1 in 42 from Plympton to Hemerdon and of no less than 57.5 m.p.h. from Totnes up to Dainton Summit; with a time of 33 min. 35 sec. over the 31.85 miles from North Road to Newton Abbot some quite considerable risks must have been taken on curves and it is very unlikely that the time of 55 min. 55 sec. for the 52.05 miles from Plymouth to Exeter will ever be repeated.

But the climax on this memorable day was the 102.3 m.p.h. attained by *City of Truro* in the descent of Wellington bank. In later years some doubt has been aroused as to the precise accuracy of Charles Rous-Marten's recording, but there can be no doubt that the speed, for the first time in British history, was in the region of 100 m.p.h. So the 128.1 miles from the Millbay station at Plymouth to Pylle Hill Junction, Bristol, were run in 123 min. 19 sec. It may be added that the Dean 4-2-2 single-driver *Duke of Connaught* achieved still further fame by covering the 118.4 miles from Pylle Hill to Paddington, with a reduced load of 120 tons, in 99 min. 46 sec., running up from Swindon in 9 sec. under the even hour and averaging precisely 80 m.p.h. over the 70.25 miles from Shrivenham to Westbourne Park. Had the run been from Temple Meads instead of Pylle Hill and unchecked, Paddington could have been reached in 98 min. from Bristol – and this by a modestly dimensioned 4-2-2 as far back as 1904!

The startling achievement of *City of Bath* with the royal special in 1903 had attracted such notice that a month later the Great Western Railway decided to put the speed capabilities of Churchward's new 4-4-0s to permanent advantage. So, in August 1903, there came into operation the first two-hour schedules between Paddington and Bristol, which with their 59.2 m.p.h. average speed were almost the fastest booked runs in Great Britain. But not quite, for the North Eastern Railway two years earlier had introduced its 43-minute run over the 44.1 miles from Darlington to York, though admittedly with a considerably lighter train.

The next Great Western timetable development of note, however, was one which put all other comparable train service demands of the period completely in the shade. It was a daily non-stop run in each direction over the 245.6 miles between Paddington and Plymouth, down in 4 hours 27 min. and up in 4 hours 25 min. To passing Bath, 106.85 miles, the time allowed was 106 min.; to Pylle Hill Junction, Bristol, 120 min.; and to passing Exeter, 193.6 miles, 197 min.; in the reverse direction the times were 195 min. from Exeter, 122 min. from Pylle Hill and 107 min. from Bath. This was a world's record at that time for length of non-stop running; and never before or since that date has a 4-4-0 locomotive been required to undertake daily continuous running on such a scale.

The train was composed of six clerestory-roofed corridor coaches and one of the new 70-ft elliptical-roofed dining cars, or a little over 200 tons in all. The French-built de Glehn compound Atlantic *La France* gave the 'City' 4-4-0s assistance in working the train, and later on the new Great Western two-cylinder Atlantics and 4-6-0s.

Two years later came the opening of the direct route to the West via Westbury; and from July of that year what had been the summer only non-stop run to Plymouth became a daily run in each direction throughout the year over a course shortened to 225.75 miles. The starting time from Paddington was altered from 10.10 a.m. to 10.30 a.m. and the train had now assumed its familiar title of 'Cornish Riviera Express'. In order to give the service a wider range of usefulness, slip portions were added, one detached at Westbury to serve the Weymouth line, and another at Exeter for the Torquay branch; and soon afterwards a third slip portion was included, to Taunton, for the benefit of passengers to Minehead and Ilfracombe. All this meant a considerable increase

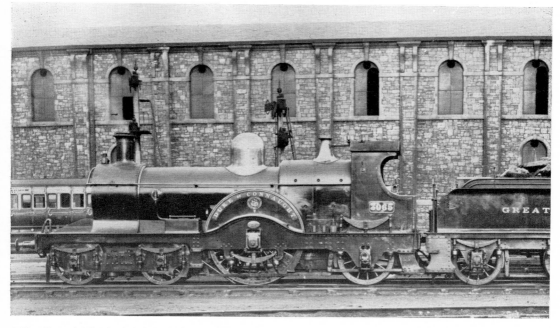

★The Dean 4-2-2 which followed *City of Truro's* 102 m.p.h. sprint with a fast Bristol–Paddington run in 1904 – No. 3065 *Duke of Connaught* at Exeter St. Davids.

★G.W. 'Star' 4-6-0 No. 4019 *Knight Templar* at the head of a 12-coach train of G.W.R. 70 ft coaches in June, 1922.          [*British Railways*]

in weight, but the first of Churchward's four-cylinder 'Star' class 4-6-0s had now come into service and they were well able to cope with the demands made by this schedule.

It was not until the year 1921 that I made my first journey by the 'Cornish Riviera Express' and the occasion is one which I am not likely to forget. By now the train had grown to twelve coaches of the heaviest 70-ft stock out of Paddington, weighing 406 tons tare and 430 tons gross; from Westbury the load came down to ten (341/360 tons), from Taunton to eight (282/295 tons) and from Exeter to seven (249/260 tons). Fog in the earlier stages and four permanent way slowings between them gave us a bad start, so much so that on passing Westbury, 95.55 miles in 107 min. 50 sec., the 'Limited' was $10\frac{1}{2}$ min. behind time. But with a completely clear road from here onwards Driver Springthorpe gave us a demonstration of what one of Churchward's four-cylinder 'Star' 4-6-0s really could do – so much so that between Westbury and Exeter alone No. 4003 *Lode Star* recovered no less than 10 min. on this fast schedule, covering the 78.15 miles in 73 min. 5 sec.

In those days 35 m.p.h. slacks had to be made round the curves through both Westbury and Frome stations, which explains the relatively low minimum speed of 49 m.p.h. at Brewham Summit, but then followed 82 m.p.h. at Bruton, $72\frac{1}{2}$ to 79 m.p.h. over the Castle Cary–Cogload cut-off, $39\frac{1}{2}$ m.p.h. minimum at Whiteball Summit and 75 to $80\frac{1}{2}$ m.p.h. down the Culm valley from Cullompton to Stoke Canon. The continuation from the 30 m.p.h. Exeter slowing was equally good; $30\frac{1}{2}$ m.p.h. at Dainton Summit and $32\frac{1}{2}$ m.p.h. minimum up Rattery bank were both creditable and by Hemerdon we were $3\frac{1}{2}$ min. ahead of time. Signal checks outside North Road – an all-too-frequent source of delay to down runs, even today – lost us a minute or two, but eventually *Lode Star* came to a stand at North Road in 244 min. 50 sec. from Paddington, just over 2 min. early; between Westbury and Lipson Junction the gain on schedule had been 16 min. Taunton had been passed in 152 min. 45 sec., Exeter in 55 sec. over 3 hours, Newton Abbot in 202 min. 20 sec., and Plympton in 236 min., but because of the signal checks the last 4.05 miles took 8 min. 50 sec. The net time on this fine run, however, had been no more than 232 min. from London and it was an exhilarating experience.

When next I travelled down to Plymouth by

the 'Cornish Riviera Express' the 'Stars' had given place to the 'Castles'; and though C. B. Collett had succeeded Churchward as Chief Mechanical Engineer at Swindon, the Churchward principles of design and the methods of handling instituted during his *régime* were still very much in evidence. By a curious coincidence, whereas my first trip by the 'Limited' was with William Springthorpe at the regulator, who had distinguished himself so greatly with *Polar Star* over London & North Western metals in the exchange trials of 1912, my second, in the autumn of 1924, was with Driver William Young and his engine *Pendennis Castle*, both to distinguish themselves equally over the London & North Eastern Railway in the historic locomotive exchange of the following year. Moreover, this time I was to have the privilege of riding with this most capable driver and Fireman Chellingworth on the footplate and not only to make their acquaintance but also that of Chief Locomotive Inspector George Flewellen, a fine character who has left behind one of the most enviable of reputations of all those who have occupied this position.

Once again the 'Cornish Riviera Express' had expanded. The train had now reached its maximum formation of 14 bogies – four for Penzance, one for St Ives, one for Falmouth and one for Plymouth; then three for Torquay, slipped at Exeter; one for Ilfracombe and one for Minehead, slipped at Taunton; and two for Weymouth, slipped at Westbury – eight different destinations in all. Tare and gross loads were thus 495/525 tons to Westbury, 423/450 tons thence to Taunton, 360/385 tons from Taunton to Exeter, and 255/275 tons over the final stage to Plymouth. For an 80-ton 4-6-0 to maintain the 'Limited' schedule in such load conditions was about as stiff a locomotive assignment as has ever been set in Great Britain.

It was a perfect autumn day and the easy competence of one of these remarkable locomotives with such a load was a revelation. The cut-off had been brought back to 33 per cent by Old Oak, to 30 by Acton and to 26 by Southall; the regulator was somewhere between two-thirds and three-quarters open; and by Slough *Pendennis Castle* was doing a steady 69 m.p.h. on the level with her 525-ton train. I wrote at the time of 'the extraordinary quietness of the exhaust.... The steady, purposeful running of this powerful locomotive was deeply impressive. I could well understand the enthusiasm with

which Mr Flewellen commended to me "her pretty beat".' In those days the original 11 min. allowance from Paddington start to Southall, 9.1 miles, laid down in the days of 250-ton train-loads at most, still remained in the working book and not surprisingly we took 2 min. more than this; but by Reading, 36.0 miles in 37 min. 50 sec., we had won back over a minute of the loss.

In the first 70 miles of this lengthy run, as far as Savernake, there is no respite for the locomotive; it is a case of steady pulling all the time and after Reading climbing begins, very gradual at first but then steepening to a final 3 miles at 1 in 175–106. The 26 per cent cut-off continued up the Kennet valley as far as Kintbury; then in stages, and still with three-quarters regulator only, cut-off was advanced finally to 30 per cent. The sensitiveness of control with one of these engines again was a revelation to me; on other locomotives I had been accustomed to see changes of 5 per cent or more at a time in cut-off positions, but here it was no more than 1 or 2 per cent and with exactly the response from the engine that the driver desired. So we kept up between 57 and 61 m.p.h. all the way from Theale to Bedwyn and only up the final pitch to Savernake did the speed drop to 48 m.p.h. Moreover, we were through Bedwyn just on the right side of schedule.

From now on the train was ahead of time the whole way. Down to Westbury cut-off came back to 17 per cent; the regulator went back to the first valve and that not fully open, until near Lavington Driver Young opened the valve to full and quickly raised the speed from $76\frac{1}{2}$ to just over 80 m.p.h. So the 'Limited' was through Westbury, 95.55 miles, in 95 min. 35 sec., or exactly 'even time'; here we shed the first two coaches of our tail. Matters were now taken fairly easily until we had cleared Taunton, 142.95 miles, in 144 min. 25 sec., with two more coaches jettisoned. Up Wellington bank, now with 385 tons, cut-off was advanced finally to 35 per cent, though still with the main regulator not fully opened, and on the final 1 in 80 speed fell to 31 m.p.h. before a reduction in speed to 25 for tunnel relining work. A swift descent of the Culm valley then took us through Exeter in 176 min. 30 sec.; round the South Devon coast the speeds were a good deal more lively than they have become under the restraints of later years, for we passed Starcross at $58\frac{1}{2}$ m.p.h. and came down to nothing lower than 50 beyond

★A close-up of G.W.R. 'Star' Class 4-6-0 No. 4026 *King Richard*.

Dawlish. Notwithstanding the handicap of a 10 m.p.h. bridge reconstruction just before Newton Abbot, we cleared that station in 200 min. 30 sec. from Paddington.

At last I saw the regulator moved to full open and though the load had now shrunk to 275 tons, even with cut-off finally advanced to 42 per cent the last 1 in 36–41 of the climb to Dainton brought speed down to 24½ m.p.h. Up Rattery bank also full regulator and 41 per cent were used for the 1 in 50 climb to Tigley box and here the lowest speed was 27 m.p.h. In those days the working timetable optimistically laid down a time of 2 min. for the tail end of the climb – the 2 miles 27 chains from Rattery to Brent, 70 m.p.h.! – and as the speed had not risen above 33 m.p.h. at the former point nor 49 at the latter, not unnaturally we lost 1 min. 20 sec. here. But all was well; the 'Limited' was still 3¼ min. early on passing Hemerdon and despite a concluding permanent way check to 25 m.p.h., we came to rest at North Road precisely 3 min. early, in 244 min. from London. The net time had been between 239 and 240 min.; on this arduous duty coal consumption had averaged no more than 34.7 lb to the mile – excluding lighting up, of course – and water a shade over 30 gallons to the mile. Such was my auspicious introduction to the 'Castles'.

It was in May of the following year, while

Driver Young and Inspector Flewellen were exercising *Pendennis Castle* to such effect over Great Northern metals, that Driver Edward Rowe made his classic run with the down 'Limited' from Paddington to Plymouth in an actual time of 231 min. 58 sec., or 230 min. net. On the same day I was travelling on the up 'Limited' behind the L.N.E.R. Pacific *Victor Wild* and we met *Caldicot Castle* just west of Starcross. As far as Exeter the latter's train was of much the same weight as on my run just previously described; but the Exeter slip was of two coaches only, leaving eight (292 tons tare and 310 tons gross) to be manoeuvred over the South Devon banks. Rowe took some distinct liberties with speed restrictions – at Reading and round the Dawlish curves in particular – but there were no particularly high maximum speeds anywhere. Reading was passed in 37 min. 25 sec., Savernake in 72 min. 25 sec., Westbury in 94 min. 40 sec., Taunton in 140 min. 30 sec., Exeter in 169 min. 10 sec. and Newton Abbot in 190 min. 25 sec. Minimum speeds were 46 m.p.h. at Savernake and 41 at Whiteball; no figures remain on record as to the times up Dainton and Rattery banks, but a time of 12 min. 40 sec. for the entire climb of 9.05 miles from Totnes to Wrangaton was a first-class effort for a 'Castle' with 310 tons at this late stage in the long run from London.

When next I travelled westwards on the

Cornish Riviera Express', in the autumn of 1927, it was once again on the footplate but for the first time on a 'King' class 4-6-0, and with the schedule cut by 7 min. to 4 hours. Though still a fourteen-coach formation, the train now carried no fewer than nine portions – four coaches for Penzance, one for St Ives, one for Falmouth, one for Newquay, one for Kingsbridge, two for Exeter (these three slipped at Exeter), one for Ilfracombe, one for Minehead and two for Weymouth. Gross weights were thus 525 tons to Westbury, 450 tons to Taunton, 380 tons to Exeter and 270 tons to Plymouth. Driver Rowse, Fireman Osborne and Chief Locomotive Inspector Robinson, who by now had succeeded George Flewellen, were my footplate companions.

The difference between the handling of a 'King' and of a 'Castle' soon became apparent. From the start the regulator was opened by degrees to full and the cut-off was brought back until by Slough it was no more than 17 per cent, with the 530-ton train travelling on the level at $62\frac{1}{2}$ m.p.h. Now followed permanent way checks at Burnham and Aldermaston, so that we were 6 min. late past Savernake, having taken 74 min. 35 sec. to this point. No more than 20 per cent cut-off up most of the Kennet valley and an advance, by 1 per cent at a time, to 24 per cent up the final 1 in 175–106, took us over the top at 49 m.p.h.

From here, 15 per cent and the small port of the regulator were sufficient to produce all but 80 m.p.h. down the 1 in 222 past Lavington and Westbury was passed in 101 min. 10 sec. As compared with the $39\frac{1}{2}$ m.p.h. of *Pendennis Castle* over Brewham Summit with 23 per cent cut-off, *King George II* went over the top at 51 m.p.h. on 25 per cent, in both cases with three-quarters regulator. Touching $80\frac{1}{2}$ m.p.h. at Bruton and 74 at Curry Rivel Junction, we were through Taunton in 146 min. 20 sec., barely 2 min. late on the accelerated schedule of $144\frac{1}{2}$ min.

Now the condition of the fire began to give some concern. Like the baskets of strawberries in the summer, the tender at Paddington had displayed a top dressing of some encouragingly large lumps of coal, but what had revealed itself as Fireman Osborne began to work his way down was something more like dust. Pressure was beginning to drop and as we forged our way up Wellington bank it was nearing the 200 lb mark; but with 35 per cent Driver Rowse took his train over Whiteball Summit at $38\frac{1}{2}$

m.p.h. Laborious use of the pricker on the fire and some nursing of the engine were now imperative, with the South Devon banks ahead, and in consequence we were 3 min. late through Exeter, in 177 min. 25 sec. from Paddington. With the lightened load, however, steady time recovery began; 35 per cent cut-off and full regulator took us over Dainton Summit at $27\frac{1}{2}$ m.p.h. and up to Tigley at a minimum of $28\frac{1}{2}$, with an increase to $43\frac{1}{2}$ m.p.h. (on 25 per cent only) on the ensuing 1 in 90 up to Rattery. So we passed Newton Abbot in 198 min. 40 sec. and came happily to a stop at North Road in 237 min. 50 sec. from Paddington, $2\frac{1}{4}$ min. early. Net time, poor coal and all, had been $233\frac{1}{2}$ min, or $6\frac{1}{2}$ min. inside schedule.

A year later I had another footplate trip with a 'King', No. 6011 *King James I*, in the charge of Driver W. Wright and Fireman Hounslow and again with Chief Locomotive Inspector Robinson. This time the trouble was not coal but cautions, *eight* of them in all, for relaying or underline bridge reconstructions – at Grafton Curve, Lavington, Cogload, Exminster, Starcross, Dawlish, Wrangaton and Redlake. We were on schedule at Bedwyn (68 min. 15 sec.), a time which, remarkable to relate, was practically a dead heat with Rowe's 68 min. 17 sec. on *Caldicot Castle* in 1925 with an identical load, but in the latter case with a higher speed round the Reading curves. On this run full regulator and 18 per cent cut-off gave us a top speed of 70 m.p.h. on the level through Slough, and between 16 and 20 per cent was used for much of the distance on to Taunton, Brewham Summit included (speed here was $50\frac{1}{2}$ m.p.h.), with maxima of $83\frac{1}{2}$ m.p.h. below Bruton and 79 at Curry Rivel Junction. Through Westbury in 98 min. 35 sec., despite the 20 m.p.h. Grafton Curve and Lavington slacks, the train was all but on time at Cogload, but a 10 m.p.h. check here put us $3\frac{1}{4}$ min. behind through Taunton (147 min. 45 sec.).

Whiteball Summit was carried at a minimum of $42\frac{1}{2}$ m.p.h. on 30 per cent cut-off, and then followed a most rousing descent towards Exeter, with 80 m.p.h. at Cullompton and 82 at Stoke Canon. My heart was in my mouth as we dashed past Cowley Bridge at 74 m.p.h. and with no indication whatever, other than shutting off steam, that we were going to slow for Exeter, where speed on all previous trips had come down to 30–40 m.p.h. But Inspector Robinson had failed to tell me (rather mischievously, I fancy) that since my last trip there had been a realignment, so that we now dropped our slip coaches short of the station and swept through Exeter at speed on the centre road at 70 m.p.h. – an electrifying experience indeed! So also was the maximum of 82 m.p.h. – the highest I have ever clocked west of Exeter – at Exminster.

At Exeter the lateness had come down to 1½ min. (175 min. 55 sec. from Paddington), but 10 m.p.h. slowings before and 20 after Starcross, followed by 5 m.p.h. at Dawlish for a bridge reconstruction, put us back once again. From Newton Abbot, passed in 201 min. 25 sec., the work was much the same as on the previous 'King' run, with cut-off increased to 35 per cent on both the major climbs, and minima of 24½ m.p.h. at Dainton and 29 at Tigley; but 25 m.p.h. permanent way slowings at Wrangaton and Redlake and a 5 m.p.h. signal check outside North Road made the total time 5 min. 35 sec. over the scheduled 4 hr. Net time was about 3 hr. 48 min.

Almost twenty years elapsed before my next footplate journey on the 'Cornish Riviera', and this was in 1947. By now there had been a radical change in the working of the express. The Second World War was only just over; as yet, while trains were very full, especially those patronized heavily by servicemen, former schedule times were far from having reappeared; the 'Limited' itself had lost all its slip portions, and its fourteen-coach load, though of less weighty stock than formerly, was working through to Plymouth; and stops were being made at Exeter and Newton Abbot. Such were the conditions when I mounted the footplate of No. 6012 *King Edward VI*, to make the acquaintance of Driver Goddard and Fireman Ball, of Laira shed (which had now taken over the working from Old Oak Common), as well as of my good friend Chief Locomotive Inspector C. J. Pullen, an expert indeed in locomotive know-how. The load was 450 tons tare and 495 tons gross.

Once again I was to be a witness of a fireman grappling with something more like coal-dust than coal, but this time on a very much easier schedule. As soon as we were into speed, 15 per cent cut-off was the order of the day, with full regulator, and similarly up the Kennet valley, save for an increase to 19 per cent to climb from Bedwyn to Savernake. There was a long permanent way slowing to 45 m.p.h. between Maidenhead and Twyford, and signals brought us down to 30 m.p.h. before Newbury. For the first time I was able to sample the Westbury and Frome cut-offs on the footplate and to realize the advantage that they gave in requiring no reduction of speed at either place. Notwithstanding the fact that at Savernake the pressure was down to 210 lb, we were 2¾ min. ahead of time past Castle Cary and could now take matters quite easily. Eventually, after breasting Whiteball Summit with our 495-ton load at 27½ m.p.h. on 25 per cent cut-off, an easy run down the Culm valley brought the 'Limited' into Exeter 3½ min. early, in 189 min. 22 sec. from Paddington.

Little needs to be said about the rest of the journey. At Newton Abbot, needless to say, we had to take assistance and as we looked down on her from the height of the 'King' footplate, 4-4-0 No. 3401 *Vancouver* as she backed down seemed quite ludicrously tiny for such an assignment. The *staccato* barks of our own exhaust up past Stoneycombe Quarries so drowned any sounds from the machine in front that it might have seemed as though we were pushing her up as well as pulling the train, but suddenly the strident puffing of the pilot came echoing back from the entry to Dainton tunnel and there was no doubt that she was valiantly doing her share. A tardy freight stowing its tail into the loop at Ivybridge stopped us at Redlake, but for all that the 'Limited' just scraped into North Road on time. One unforgettable experience of this particular trip was the colour of my companions and myself on alighting. I well remember leaning out of the cab as we wound our way round the sea wall at Dawlish and comparing my visage with the nice pink bathers lying on the sand below. When Driver Goddard tooted on his whistle as we passed Laira to let his wife know at their nearby house that he was safely back, I told him not to forget to tell her the identity of the two distinguished African potentates that he had on the footplate with him!

Finally I come to two 'Cornish Riviera Express' runs in which it was my privilege to travel, not on the footplate, but in the dynamometer car, where in the greatest comfort one can see at a glance not merely all that is happening on the footplate, but also at any moment of the run the drawbar pull, the drawbar horsepower and many other most interesting details of the performance. The company of such an expert as Mr S. O. Ell, Assistant to the W.R. Chief Mechanical Engineer for Locomotive Testing, and of his staff also ensured that the observer was going to have trips that were both entertaining and enlightening. The particular interest of these journeys was that the work of No. 6002 *King William IV*, brought right up to date with thirty-two-element superheater, double blastpipe and double chimney, was being compared with that of the London Midland Region Pacific No. 46237 *City of Bristol*, specially loaned for the purpose. The L.M.R. engine was being worked by a Western Region crew, Driver Harris and Fireman Tobin of Old Oak; the W.R. 'King' was manned by Driver Powell and Fireman Shave, also of Old Oak; both crews were accompanied on the footplate by Chief Locomotive Inspector Andress, and both engines were using coal from a Welsh pit named Markham.

I will not dwell on the down journeys, as the 'King' was badly delayed by a 23 min. stop because of wagons off the line at Patney and wrong line working thence to Lavington, as well as a 4 min. signal stop at Southcote Junction and five other signal and permanent way checks; in consequence we reached Newton Abbot 40 min. late. Net time, however, with a fourteen-coach load of 490 tons to Westbury

and twelve of 420 tons thence, was not more than $176\frac{1}{2}$ min. for the 193.7 miles – considerably less than on any of the runs previously described. On the level at Slough 15 per cent cut-off and full regulator gave a speed of 73 m.p.h., with the engine developing a drawbar h.p. of 1,150 and a drawbar pull of about 6,000 lb. Over Brewham Summit speed was as high as $64\frac{1}{2}$ m.p.h., and we touched 86 m.p.h. at Curry Rivel; minimum at Whiteball tunnel was 47 m.p.h., the drawbar h.p. here mounting to 1,400. The highest drawbar h.p. reached was on Rattery bank, after No. 6948 *Holbrooke Hall* had been attached at Newton Abbot to assist; here the figure rose to 1,550. For the whole journey the average was 1,000 to 1,250 drawbar h.p. continuously, for a coal consumption averaging 42.5 lb to the mile. The work of the Stanier Pacific was very similar; one slight superiority of the latter was the $76\frac{1}{2}$ m.p.h. attained on the level at Slough, but her net time to Newton Abbot was $181\frac{3}{4}$ min., $5\frac{1}{4}$ min. more than that of *King William IV*.

The major interest attaches, however, to the

(*Concluded on page* 58)

★'Castle' Class 4-6-0 No. 5078 *Beaufort* leaves Teignmouth and skirts the sea wall with the 8 a.m. Plymouth-Crewe in August, 1956. [*R. J. Blenkinsop*

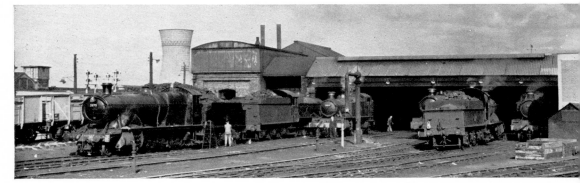

**Left:** On a July Saturday in 1959, 'King' 4-6-0 No. 6018 *King Henry VI* double-heads Type N.B. Loco. Co. '4' diesel No. D602 *Bulldog* out of Newton Abbot towards the South Devon banks on the 10.35 a.m. Paddington–Plymouth.

# The last days of steam at NEWTON ABBOT

**Photographed by D. S. FISH**

**Centre left:** A general view of Newton Abbot shed in September, 1959.

**Bottom left:** The 1.25 p.m. Paddington–Kingswear passes Hackney goods yard behind 2-8-0 No. 4706 and approaches Newton Abbot East signalbox on July, 4 1959.

**Above:** The down 'Torbay Express' passes through Newton Abbot non-stop in October, 1959 with 'Castle' Class 4-6-0 No. 7017 *G. J. Churchward* in charge.

**Below:** Summer Saturday afternoon rush-hour in July, 1959, with a 'Britannia' Pacific leaving for the west; two other westbound expresses, both headed by 'Castle' Class 4-6-0s, wait for the road behind it.

*(Concluded from page 55)*
up journeys. The aim was to reach Paddington by 4.30 p.m., 10 min. earlier than the normal arrival of the 'Limited' at that time and with a twelve-coach load of 393 tons tare and 420 tons gross, which called for double-heading from Plymouth to Newton Abbot. It was after Exeter, passed 2 min. late, that Driver Newcombe and Fireman Walker of Laira set *King William IV* to work to some purpose. Up the 1 in 115 to Whiteball the lowest speed was 50½ m.p.h., and then followed 88 m.p.h. down Wellington bank; high speed continued to Curry Rivel (77½ m.p.h.), a minimum of 66 m.p.h. up the 1 in 264 to Somerton tunnel, 49 m.p.h. at Brewham (after climbing the series of 1 in 98–81 inclinations that extend over some 4½ miles), and 75–80 m.p.h. over the Frome and Westbury cut-offs. Between Exeter and Heywood Road Junction there was a clear gain of 13½ min. on schedule and speed averaged 73.5 m.p.h. over the 66.7 miles from Whiteball to Lavington. At several points the drawbar h.p. rose to 1,400.

A bad permanent way check was experienced before Patney and slight signals at the approach to Savernake; from here onwards matters were taken more easily, but despite an extremely slow entry to the terminus Paddington was reached in 188 min. 25 sec. from Newton Abbot home signals (a distance of 194.1 miles) or 182 min. net. From Plymouth, including 2 min. standing at Newton, we had taken 3 hr. 55 min. 41 sec. Net times from Exeter and Taunton to London were 157½ and 128½ min. for the 173.5 and 142.75 miles respectively – a remarkable performance.

The Pacific *City of Bristol*, in charge of Driver Emery and Fireman Harris of Laira, was worked rather more easily in the early stages, being 2½ min. behind the 'King' at Taunton and then delayed by a 27 m.p.h. permanent way check at Athelney; but the minimum speed of 52 m.p.h. up the climb to Brewham was notable – indeed, this was the first time I have ever recorded over 50 m.p.h. in this direction with such a load. The Frome and Westbury cut-offs were taken at a lower speed than on the 'King' run, but then came an acceleration on the level from 73 m.p.h. at Heywood Road Junction to no less than 80 before reaching the foot of Lavington bank, on which the permanent way slowing was even more severe than on the previous run. By Twyford it was clear that we should have to hurry to be in Paddington by 4.30 p.m., but hurry we did, getting up to 80 m.p.h. on the level from Slough to West Drayton and rolling to a stand with just 7 sec. to spare!

From Plymouth, including 1¾ min. at Newton Abbot, the time had been almost precisely 4 hr. and the net time 3 hr. 48 min.; we had run up from Newton Abbot in 193 min. 45 sec. or 183 min. net; the net times from Exeter and Taunton had been 157½ and 126½ min. respectively, almost identical with those of the 'King', and with similar maximum drawbar h.p. readings of 1,400 or so. Such has been the history of steam locomotive running between Paddington and Plymouth which with the Great Western 'Castles' and 'Kings' has been consistently in the highest tradition of British locomotive performance. Since then I have made several runs on the 'Limited' on or behind diesel-hydraulic locomotives, but the thrill is never quite the same as it used to be in the halcyon days of steam.

# Manchester Victoria and Exchange

## By G. RICHARD PARKES

★Rebuilt 'Patriot' 4-6-0 No. 45525 *Colwyn Bay* pulls out of Manchester Exchange with the 9 a.m. Newcastle-Liverpool.     [K. Field

● A rail-tour in text and picture of one of Britain's largest provincial traffic centres —and the home of the country's longest platform.

VICTORIA and Exchange stations have always been closely linked – in fact, Exchange was built because there came a time when Victoria could no longer cope with the traffic. But there were railways in Manchester before Victoria came into being. The Liverpool & Manchester Railway, the first to haul passenger traffic by steam, which was opened in 1830, had its first Manchester terminus at Liverpool Road; the buildings are still there today, mostly in their original form. The Manchester & Leeds Railway, opened throughout in 1841, built its terminus at Oldham Road and this elevated structure, coming to an end in the middle of Oldham Road goods depot, is still there, too, although it is no longer used for passenger traffic.

The inconvenience for passengers of having to cross Manchester and the difficulties of transhipping goods from one railway to another led to the Liverpool & Manchester and the Manchester & Leeds Railways extending their routes to meet near Hunt's Bank. The M.&L.R. constructed a line from Miles Platting, about a mile above the Oldham Road station, down a steep incline (1 in 47 and 1 in 59) some 2,320 yds. long to a point near Hunt's Bank; and the L.&M.R. built a line on arches from Ordsall Lane, fairly close to their Liverpool Road station, to the same place. Victoria station was erected at the convergence and opened in 1844. With an overall length of 852 ft., it was at that time the largest station in the country.

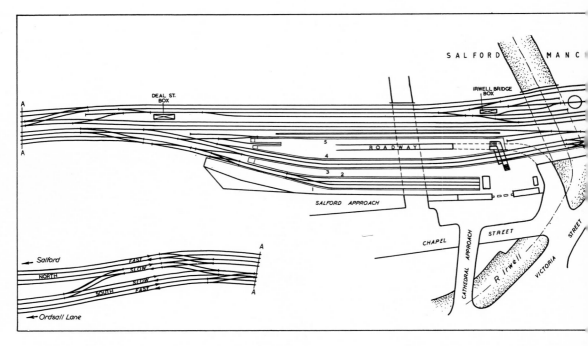

At first, the line from Victoria to Miles Platting was worked by a stationary engine hauling trains up the incline by means of a wire rope. The trains descended by their own momentum, their speed regulated by a brake wagon, loaded with several tons of ballast, which was placed in front of the carriages. This rope haulage continued until 1846, by which time the locomotives were powerful enough to pull trains up the incline without assistance. In 1877, a new line was opened from Victoria via Cheetham Hill to Thorpes Bridge Junction beyond Miles Platting, which enabled some important expresses to avoid the steep incline. Nowadays the heaviest trains, both freight and passenger, are assisted up the incline by either a pilot or a banker.

By 1880, traffic movement in Victoria station was becoming very congested and the L.N.W.R. decided to build its own Exchange station. At the same time, the L.&Y.R., the successor of the M.&L.R., undertook a substantial extension of Victoria in the form of terminal platforms for certain suburban services. Exchange station was opened in the same year that the extensions in Victoria were completed – 1884. Up to that time Victoria had been the joint property of the L.&Y.R. and the L.N.W.R., but now the station became exclusively an

L.&Y.R. concern, although the L.N.W.R. retained running rights through Victoria, particularly for their expresses to Leeds, Newcastle and Hull.

In 1862, the two companies came to an agreement which eliminated much overlapping and provided for the pooling of competitive traffics; this agreement was renewed from time to time until 1904, when a much broader pool was negotiated. Indeed, these two railways concluded an agreement for their complete amalgamation from January 1, 1872, subject to the necessary approval of Parliament; but, although the shareholders of both companies enthusiastically adopted the scheme, the Bill encountered so much opposition that the plan had to be dropped. After the first World War, the 50-year friendship between the L.N.W.R. and the L.&Y.R. progressed a stage further by the appointment from January 1, 1921 of Sir Arthur Watson as General Manager of both railways. Three months later it was officially announced that complete amalgamation was pending, but the subsequent passage of the Railways Act, 1921, resulted in the merger ranking as a preliminary 'grouping' scheme.

Broadly speaking, both Victoria and Exchange stations are the same now as they were in 1884. The only major change, apart from

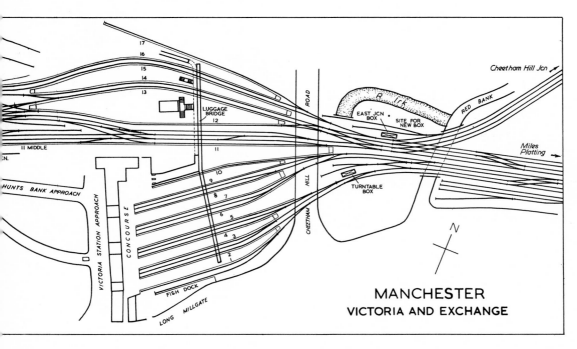

**MANCHESTER**
**VICTORIA AND EXCHANGE**

track and signalling alterations, has been the elimination of three short sidings on the main bridge and the joining of Platforms 11 at Victoria and 3 at Exchange in place of the sidings. Most of the other changes of structure were due, in the main, to enemy action during the war. Exchange was heavily bombed on December 22, 1940. All the lines were blocked and, although by January 1, 1941 one up and one down line were available for trains not stopping at the station, the station itself was not reopened for pasenger service until January 13 – and then for a limited amount of traffic only. On December 23, most of the buildings on Platforms 12 to 17 at Victoria were either totally destroyed or extensively damaged. The damage also included the total destruction of the Divisional Control Office and many of the Divisional Superintendent's offices. The Emergency Control Office, which had been provided to cover possible loss of the Divisional Office, was flooded and the control telephone communications put out of action. Thus the nerve centre of the system in this large Division was temporarily knocked out. Reactions were widespread, especially in Lancashire, Yorkshire and Derbyshire, and were particularly serious within a 30-mile radius. Victoria lost about half the roof over Platforms 12 to 17 and it has

never been replaced. The roof over Exchange has been renewed, but the buildings have not.

Today Victoria has 17 platforms and the station is used by some 8½m. passengers a year. Exchange has 5 platforms which are used by nearly 3m. passengers yearly. The longest platform in the country, 2,194 ft., is known as No. 11; actually it comprises Victoria's No. 11, No. 11 Middle (which joins Victoria to Exchange) and Exchange No. 3.

Manchester Victoria deals with some 320 arrivals and 310 departures of ordinary passenger trains on weekdays and in addition with close on 40 passenger and 40 freight trains passing through the station. The peak hour for arrivals is between 8 a.m. and 9 a.m., when 40 trains are received in the station; in the evening rush between 5 and 6 p.m., there is a similar total of departures. The daily totals I have quoted include 79 arrivals and 77 departures on the Bury electric line.

The principal routes served from Victoria are those to Liverpool, Wigan, Southport, Preston, Blackpool and Fleetwood; to Bolton, Blackburn, Hellifield; to Bury, Bacup, Accrington and Colne; to Oldham, Rochdale, Todmorden, Halifax, Bradford and Leeds; to Wakefield, Normanton, Goole and York; and to Stalybridge and Stockport (for Euston). The

★The facade of Manchester Victoria; note the legend 'Lancashire & Yorkshire Railway' in the stonework under the clock.                                                    [K. Field

★The concourse of Manchester Victoria – a view in April, 1960.                                                    [G. R. Parkes

old Lancashire & Yorkshire Railway was renowned for its long-distance commuter services connecting Manchester with Southport, Blackpool and Fleetwood (these fast and reliable trains are still used by hundreds of travellers today), but in the main the workings from Victoria connect the closely-knit towns of the heavily industrialized areas in Lancashire and the West Riding of Yorkshire. Most of them start or terminate at Victoria, but there

are some through services – for example, those between Liverpool, Manchester, Bradford and Leeds via the Calder Valley, which from the beginning of 1962 were reorganized into a regular-interval service on an hourly basis for operation by new Birmingham R.C.& W. Co. three-car diesel multiple-units.

The station's capacity was taxed to the limit in 1960. In that year, during the final stages of the reconstruction of London Road into the new, steamless Manchester Piccadilly, Victoria had to accommodate numerous trains which do not usually go there. From January 4 to April 24, six trains daily each way from the ex-Great Central line used Victoria, travelling via Ashburys, Phillips Park and Miles Platting. The change-over from electric to steam traction, and *vice versa*, took place at Midland

★The map of the old Lanchashire & Yorkshire stystem in tiles which survives in Manchester Victoria station.
                                                    [K. Field

**Right:** A four-car Cravens diesel multiple-unit bound for Bury via the main line climbs Miles Platting bank out of Manchester Victoria.

[*K. Field*

**Above:** A view towards Manchester Victoria from the Newton Heath direction; the Class '5' 4-6-0 in the foreground is coming off that shed to work a train from Manchester Victoria. On the left is Red Bank coaching stock yard.

[*K. Field*

**Right:** 'Crab' 2-6-0 No. 42789 descends Miles Platting bank and approaches Manchester Victoria with an excursion. The new central signalbox has been erected beyond the old structure on the left.

[*K. Field*

★The west end of Manchester Victoria, with a Cravens diesel multiple-unit for Bolton leaving on the extreme left and 'Crab' 2-6-0 No. 42868 on an empty stock working in the foreground. [K. Field

Junction, where the Midland spur from Ashburys meets the Ardwick Branch from London Road. From April 22 to September 12, Birmingham trains were diverted to depart from Victoria, via Miles Platting, Droylsden, Heaton Norris and Stockport, and on to Crewe.

Victoria is fronted by a magnificent block of office buildings, with a canopy covering the pavement for almost the full length of the approach and protecting three of the main entrances into the station concourse. There is a fourth entrance from Long Millgate. The concourse runs the full length of the 'new' part of the station behind the ends of Platforms 1 to 10 and the entrance to Platforms 11 to 17, and finishes at Platform 11. The whole of the concourse and Platforms 1 to 11 are covered by a glazed roof. On or adjoining the concourse are the usual features of any large station—booking office, information bureau, cafeteria, refreshment room, left luggage office, bookstalls, tobacco and sweet kiosks, and so on. At the north end of the concourse, on the right just past the information bureau, is the entrance to Platforms 11 to 17. Through the barrier to the

left is Platform 11 and further left still is Platform 11 Middle, leading to Exchange; straight ahead of the barrier is a subway to the remaining platforms.

Of the 25 tracks in Victoria, the first road is the Fish Dock, which is walled off from the passenger station. Every weekday, except Monday, a fish train arrives here from Aberdeen; it comes off the up passenger loop outside Exchange at 8.52 a.m., passes through Victoria to the Millgate signalbox and sets back into the Fish Dock. Platforms 1, 2, and 3 are used by the electric services to Bury. Platforms 4 to 10 accommodate trains to Oldham, Royton, Rochdale, Bacup, Stalybridge and so on, via Miles Platting. Some of these local services use Platform 3 as well and nearly all today are diesel multiple-units.

The track which serves Platform No. 11 branches off the up main line opposite the East Junction signalbox and runs right through Victoria to Exchange, where it is known as the Down Platform No. 3. It may be well to explain here that all roads leading to Manchester on the L.Y.R. were 'up', and those going away

A Cravens diesel multiple-unit from Bolton at Platform 12 of Manchester Victoria; on the right are the through tracks between the two stations with 'Britannia' Pacific No. 70043 Lord Kitchener in the background. [K. Field

**Right:** 'Britannia' Pacific No. 70050 *Firth of Clyde* at the continuous platform linking Victoria and Exchange stations on the 9.30 a.m. express to Glasgow. [K. Field

**Above:** A view across the layout at the west end of Manchester Victoria from the platform linking the two stations; ex-L.Y.R. 0-6-0 No. 52275 is on banking duty (a job these engines no longer perform) and the diesel multiple-unit on the extreme right is bound for Blackpool. [K. Field

**Right:** In the days before this service was taken over by diesel multiple-units, 'Jubilee' 4-6-0 No. 45581 *Bihar and Orissa* crosses from the through road to the platform in Manchester Exchange with the 9 a.m. Hull–Liverpool express. [K. Field

**Above:** Banked in rear for the ascent of Miles Platting bank, 'Patriot' Class 4-6-0 No. 45502 *Royal Naval Division* (now withdrawn) leaves Manchester Exchange and takes the through line past Manchester Victoria with a Leeds relief in June, 1960.　　　[*T. Lewis*

**Below:** Another view of the through roads of Manchester Victoria, with a Class 'WD' 2-8-0 returning the Newton Heath breakdown train to its home; on the right is ex-L.Y.R. 0-6-0 No. 52328 on the banking duty these engines used to perform.　　　[*K. Field*

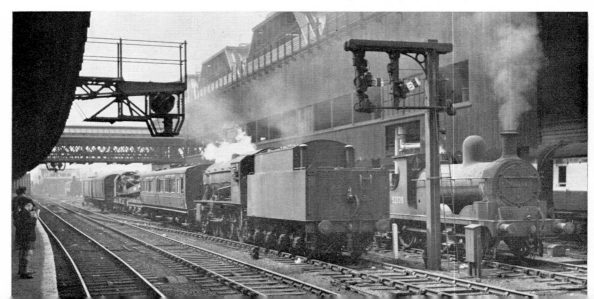

from the city were 'down'; thus one changes from up to down when passing from Exchange from Victoria. The track serving Platform No. 11 can be entered at two other places – from the up main line at the end of the platform and at the beginning of Platform 11 Middle, and from the down through line (which continues the up through and the up main) at the entrance to Exchange. This means that three trains can use this platform, the longest in the country, at the same time; and any one of the three trains can get into or out of their section of the platform without interfering with the other two. Platform 11 is particularly useful in emergencies or on special occasions. For example, on August Bank Holiday in 1959 a coach was derailed at the east end of Platform 12, blocking the tracks to Platforms, 12, 13 and 14. Westbound trains which should have used any of those three platforms were switched to Platform 11 and the maximum delay to any of them was ten minutes; most of them were dispatched with only four minutes' delay.

Beyond Platform 11 are two through roads. The first – the up main, becomes the up through and then the down through; trains on this track can switch to Platform 11, 11 Middle or Exchange No. 3, they can continue on the down through line in Exchange station, or they can switch to the down slow just before the West Junction signalbox to avoid Exchange altogether. The through road in the opposite direction is the up slow line past Exchange and runs parallel to the up passenger loop. On reaching Victoria it becomes the down through line and is joined by the up roads from Platforms 4 and 5 of Exchange, which, as they leave Exchange, become down tracks. The up passenger loop joins the road from Platform 5 just before the West Junction signalbox. These two through roads are used by freight traffic and by passenger trains which do not stop at Victoria.

Platform 12 is used for arrivals from the east and departures to the west, although on occasions, it is employed for traffic departing to the east. Platforms 13 to 16 are used for trains arriving or departing in either direction. It is not unusual, for instance, to find two trains at the same platform, say No. 15, which are departing in opposite directions. Platform No. 17, a dead-end, is used for parcels traffic exclusively, except for one Friday night passenger train to Todmorden, for about two months in the summer.

Exchange Station, nominally in Manchester but actually within Salford, used to have quite an imposing frontage, in some ways not unlike the former London Road before its transformation into Manchester Piccadilly. Unhappily, the station was blitzed in the last war and now it has a plain and rather drab-looking brick wall. The main entrance is at the top of the Cathedral approach. The ticket offices and information office are outside the barriers, which lead directly on to the concourse; the refreshment room was destroyed in the war and there is now a stall on the concourse where light refreshments may be obtained. On Platform 1 there is a staff canteen, which provides good meals at very reasonable prices; it is sometimes used by passengers on the night train to Glasgow and Edinburgh as there is nowhere else to get a cup of tea at that time of night.

The main services of Exchange are long-distance through trains, particularly between Liverpool Lime Street and Hull or Newcastle, both via Huddersfield and Leeds. The former are now provided by the 'Trans-Pennine' diesel multiple-unit, the latter are Type '4' diesel-hauled expresses. Exchange is the gateway to Chester and North Wales. The 4.30 p.m. to Llandudno used to be known as 'The Club Train'. It still has the same businessmen's character – and woe betide any stranger who inadvertently takes the seat of a 'regular'; the least he is likely to get is a very dirty look. The inward 'club' train leaves Llandudno at 7.40 a.m. and is due in Exchange at 9.57 a.m. There are also through services to Barrow and Windermere and stopping services on the routes to Leeds, Wigan, Liverpool and Chester. In all, there are about 60 arrivals and 60 departures daily.

In 1928 there were radical alterations in both track layout and signalling at Victoria and Exchange. Previously, there was no physical connection between four lines from the west end of Victoria which passed through Exchange and the four lines departing from the west end of Exchange. These groups of lines were known as the North and South lines respectively. It was decided to install crossovers between the South slow and the North slow lines. The advantage of these arrangements was that, while the North lines continued to serve mainly Platforms 11 to 16 in Victoria, they also connected with all those in Exchange. Similarly, in addition to the South lines access to all the platforms in Exchange, they were connected also

**Right:** One of Newton Heath's 'Britannia' Pacifics, No. 70048 *The Territorial Army 1908–1958*, rounds the curve out of Manchester Exchange and heads towards Salford with freight in June, 1960.

*[J. R. Carter*

**Below:** 'Britannia' Pacific No. 70052 *Firth of Tay* is piloted out of Manchester with the 9.30 a.m. Glasgow express by Class '4' 2-6-4T No. 42655 in November, 1961.

*[J. R. Carter*

Two views of the western exit from Manchester Exchange, showing (**right**) 'Jubilee' 4-6-0 No. 45553 *Canada* on the 5.10 p.m. to Windermere in August, 1960; and Caprotti Class '5' 4-6-0 No. 44686 on the 4.30 p.m. Llandudno 'Club train', in July, 1960.

*[J. R. Carter*

★A bird's eye view of the west end of Manchester Exchange in April, 1960; Victoria can be dimly seen in the left background.                    [G. R. Parkes

with all those in Victoria. As a consequence, trains could leave Victoria for destinations served by the South lines – for example, North Wales – and could depart from Exchange for all places in the North and West for which Victoria only was generally used.

All the signalboxes in the area at that time were mechanical and the signals were of the semaphore type. It was decided to install four-aspect colour-light signals and power-operated points; this was the first major installation of its kind outside the London area. Originally there were ten signalboxes. These were replaced by three power-worked boxes – Deal Street, Victoria West Junction and Irwell Bridge Sidings –

and three mechanical boxes – Ordsall Lane, Salford and Victoria East Junction – from which a considerable number of mechanical levers were removed. Route indicators, for low-speed movements, are of the Westinghouse optical-projector type; these have no moving parts, the image being projected on to a glass screen.

A new signalbox has been erected behind the Victoria East Junction box and was completed in the spring of 1962. It replaces the previous East Junction, Turntable, Millgate, Newtown No. 1 and No. 2, Footbridge, and Cheetham Hill Junction boxes. Colour-light signalling has been installed for operation from this new cabin.

# The Kiruna-Narvik iron ore railway

## by NOEL WATTS

★A Kiruna–Narvik iron ore train between Kattejokk and Riksgransen, near the Norwegian–Swedish border.

● A heavily occupied electric railway moves 15 million tons of mineral traffic a year across the Arctic Circle.

MANY of the world's railways owe their inception to man's insatiable demand for minerals. The great 'Ore Line', as the Swedes call it, which runs through the heart of Lapland, in northern Scandinavia, is one of them – in fact, its construction played a vital role in the development of the vast iron ore fields of Arctic Sweden. It had been known for several hundred years previously that there were large deposits of iron in the Gällivare area and small ironworks were active there; but, owing to their remote situation, it was almost impossible to transport more than a small quantity of their products to seaports on the Gulf of Bothnia. Although Gällivare is just on the Arctic Circle and nearly 200 miles from the sea at Luleå, early accounts of the work in the ore fields show that attempts were made to transport iron on sledges drawn by reindeer and driven by Lapps.

Then, in 1890, an incredible 'mountain of iron' was discovered at Kiruna. Once the real magnitude of this deposit became known, serious plans were laid to develop it and other neighbouring finds. The ore company estimates that the deposit contains in one mountain 1,300 million tons of high grade ore, which has up to 70 per cent of iron in its constitution. This means, incidentally, that the ore is extremely dense and that therefore wagon loadings are very heavy. This high density (nearly as great as that of pure iron) also poses a problem for the shippers at Narvik. When a ship is loaded, nearly one-third of its volume must be left empty to provide sufficient buoyancy to float the vessel.

The problems which beset the firms who attempted to develop the area were numerous and severe. Kiruna lies about 100 miles north of the Arctic Circle in a land which will grow little except small birch trees and which has a winter lasting from late September to the end of May. Winter temperatures average minus 4° Fahrenheit – frequently there are 60° of frost – and the whole land lies deeply under snow. In addition there are months of semi-darkness and for seven or eight weeks the sun does not rise at all.

The first concession for mining and railway construction at Gällivare was granted to an English company. They built a railway to the port of Luleå on the Gulf of Bothnia, which was moderately successful. But Luleå has the fatal disadvantage of being ice-bound for many months each year and it was realized at once that the Kiruna project would succeed only if an ice-free port could be found.

This would, of necessity, have to be to the west, on the coast of Norway where the Gulf Stream prevents ice forming as far north as the North Cape. After a series of surveys the point where the town of Narvik now stands was chosen as the most suitable place for the construction of a port. It is 100 miles from Kiruna, where the land rises gently to the mountains which form the boundary between Sweden and

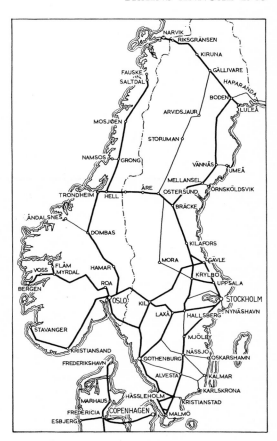

Norway; beyond this range the ground falls sharply from a height of about 2,000 ft to sea-level in 20 miles. The English company attempted to build their line along the survey route and proposed to power it with steam locomotives, but the return gradient from Narvik proved too much for the locomotives available. Before replacements could be obtained the company ran into financial difficulties and went bankrupt; in 1889, therefore, all work on the railway was abandoned. Nothing more was done until ten years later, when a new Swedish iron-ore company was formed (known throughout Scandinavia as LKAB*) and the Swedish and Norwegian Governments under-

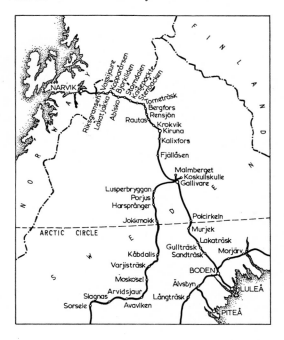

* LKAB Luossavaara-Kirunavaara Aktiebolaget. (Named after Kiruna's twin mountains). It owns the mines and the installation at Narvik, it has its own fleet of ore boasts and its own hotel for its ships' captains and crews in Narvik. Immensely rich, it plays an enormous part in Sweden's economy and since 1957 has been fully nationalised.

*Above:* 'Royal Scot' 4-6-0 No. 46120 *Royal Iniskilling Fusilier* approaches Beechwood Tunnel, near Berkeswell, with a Wolverhampton–Euston express on April 16, 1961.

**Photographed by M. MENSING**

*Below:* The 3.33 p.m. Wolverhampton–Paddington express between Widney Manor and Knowle & Dorridge behind W.R. 4-6-0 No. 6022 *King Edward III* on July 9, 1961.

A panorama of the Clapham Junction layout at the London end of the station. The steam train in the left background is an Oxted–Victoria service headed by a B.R. Class '4' 2-6-4T. In the left foreground a 'Merchant Navy' 4-6-2 on the up 'Bournemouth Belle' is about to pass a Portsmouth-bound electric multiple-unit. In the right foreground is 'Battle of Britain' 4-6-2 No. 34087 *145 Squadron*, and behind it are the Windsor line platforms.

**From a painting by TERENCE CUNEO**

By courtesy of British Railways
Southern Region

*Above:* Class 'A1' 4-6-2 No. 60136 *Alcazar* approaches Sandy with a morning express from the West Riding to Kings Cross on August 7, 1961.

**Photographed by M. MENSING**

*Below:* Class 'V2' 2-6-2 No. 60897 crosses to the up main line north of Sandy with the 9.56 a.m. Peterborough–Kings Cross semi-fast on August 7, 1961.

took the construction of the railway from Kiruna to Narvik.

Tremendous activity ensued. The towns of Kiruna and Narvik were built (in 1900 there was just one farm where Narvik now stands, and nothing at all on the site of Kiruna, except for the surveyors' huts) and within three years the railway to Narvik was completed. The first ore trains reached the newly constructed quays on November 15, 1902, and the flow has increased year by year since then. In the first twelve months one million tons of iron ore were exported. By 1958 this annual quantity had risen to 10 million tons and to date over 200 million tons of ore have been transported over the mountains on the ore line.

When the ore quays were originally built they were so designed that each wagon's contents were tipped separately down a chute into a ship waiting beneath. This was a slow, cumbersome process and as the years passed various methods of speeding up the loading were evolved. Then, in the last war, when iron was vital to munition work, Narvik became a key point in the struggle. In the various battles which were fought there, and as a result of the 'scorched earth' policies, almost the whole town and harbour installations had been destroyed by the end of the war. In 1947 the place presented a sorry sight, but immediate plans were put in hand to rebuild and modernize the whole loading plant and the many miles of railway sidings. Millions of pounds were spent – ironically enough with a German firm – on the new piers, at which it is possible to berth two ships and load them simultaneously at the rate of 4,500 tons an hour. Complete ore trains are run into sidings where the whole load is tipped simultaneously into vast 'bins', from which it is picked up by conveyors and belts several kilometres long and passed directly to the ships. From the mines to the boats the whole process is completely mechanized and trains are turned round in a very short space of time.

The first 23 miles of the line are in Norway and, although no other Norwegian railway is nearer than 150 miles, this short piece of route forms part of the Norwegian State Railways. It is called the Ofoten Line, after the Norwegian province in which it is situated. Bright green electric locomotives of the Norwegian State Railways head a number of the ore trains and work right through from Narvik to Kiruna. This Norwegian section of the line is one of the most spectacular in the world and the

views it offers over the fjords are magnificent.

About a mile from the ore quays is Narvik passenger station. This, like the rest of the town, is new and a most comfortable and well-appointed place. As explained later, it handles a very considerable passenger traffic, for anyone wishing to visit the north of Norway catches the mail steamers here; the State Railways estimate that over 120,000 people pass through Narvik station in a year – a remarkable total in view of its remoteness. Soon after leaving the station the railway reaches the south shore of Rombaks Fiord, where a stone memorial commemorates the official opening of the line by the King of Norway in July, 1903. At that time this was the most northerly point in the world reached by a railway – 68½ deg. N. latitude.

Immediately the line starts to climb up the almost sheer cliffs which line the fjord, through cuttings, tunnels, show-sheds and sections cut on the open face of the cliff. Rombaks station, at the head of the fjord, is just 1,000 ft above the sea and for some years after the last war it was possible to look straight down from here on the wrecks of the German destroyers and submarines shattered in the battle of Narvik. Beyond Rombaks the line still climbs and curves sharply through more tunnels, crossing the narrow Norddal Valley on a bridge 200 yds long and 140 ft above the river, before it reaches Björnfell, the last station in Norway, 1,750 ft above sea-level and well above the tree line.

I had the opportunity to appreciate the remoteness of this wild spot a few years ago when the Narvik–Kiruna train in which I was travelling developed engine trouble just short of the entrance to a snow-shed on this climb. It was late in August, with the nights shortening, and a mixture of rain and snow was falling: only the dripping water broke the eerie silence outside the train. The driver attempted to restart by letting the train slide back some yards and then switching on the power. He had a heavy load, for this was the Stockholm train, and it was packed with passengers. Each vain attempt deepened worried looks among the passengers until the guard came along to announce that help had been sent for. Each snow-shed is equipped with a telephone and another locomotive had been called up. There was great relief when its whistle was heard booming through the snow-shed and even more when its great headlight slowly appeared out of the gloom, whereupon the train was soon on its way.

After crossing the frontier at Riksgransen, the

**Left:** Abisko station, half-way from Kiruna to Narvik, in the spring. The large building with the tower at the rear of the station building (the clock is just discernible) is one of the transformer houses mentioned in the article. The whole transformer unit can be withdrawn on rails through the double doors and taken away for servicing; stand-by units can be substituted in a few hours. The other houses are those of railway workers.

**Above:** Narvik station, like the town, was completely destroyed during the war. The photograph shows the new station completed in 1950.              [C. E. N. Watts

**Below:** Polcirkeln station on the Arctic Circle; the name means 'Pole Circle'.

**Above:** Kiruna station is modern and well-appointed.

**Below:** A station high above Rombaks fjord. The stationmaster's rostrum, from which he supervises the handling of trains by his station, can be seen on the extreme right.

✶A view over the town of Kiruna looking towards the largest ore mine. The great hole which has taken fifty years to dig can be seen very clearly.

line makes a gradual descent to Kiruna, 80 miles farther on. Once the border is crossed the country is very lovely during the short Arctic summer. The line passes a succession of beautiful lakes, including the whole 40 miles' length of Lake Torne (Tornetrask). Here an extensive tourist trade has been built up and summer hotels line the route; at midsummer the sun does not set on them for nearly seven weeks. In this section of the line is Sweden's longest railway tunnel. It is bored under the mountain called Nuolja and is 1,052 m. (slightly over 3,000 ft) long.

★Wagons of ore about to be tipped on to conveyor belts at Narvik harbour.

On this route the engineers' main difficulties arise from the swamps, innumerable lakes and water courses liable to severe flooding and, above all, from the extreme weather conditions which call for constant vigilance and preparations to meet all emergencies. To avoid swamps the line takes a devious route with what seem to British eyes very severe curves. But the articulated locomotives take the sharpest of them with little or no reduction of speed – indeed, it is

★One of the electric locomotives working in the iron ore mines at Kiruna.

fascinating to look forward from the train and see the track winding its way like a snake through the countryside, then feel the train take to the nicely banked curves without any change of speed.

Much of the line is built on sandy subsoil and subsidences are frequent, sometimes with expensive consequences. In our travels we noticed near Abisko that there was a speed restriction and work seemed to be going on to strengthen the track. Three days later the express we were travelling in over the same stretch of track was halted. We were told that the train ahead was

★This picture illustrates dramatically the conditions with which the operating staff have to cope in winter on the Kiruna–Narvik railway. An electric locomotive is propelling a rotary snowplough.

derailed and that we must walk past the wreck to a point where a relief would pick us up. Everything from our train had to be carried for half a mile past the obstruction, which appeared to be a large plough of some sort. At 6 a.m. on a wet morning it was not at all a pleasant experience to have to carry one's luggage through wet clinging sand! We were delayed for two hours, but before Boden was reached (300 miles away) the time lost had been made up.

★In winter the frozen Swedish iron ore must be thawed out before loading on to ships can begin. Sometimes, as in this case, steam is piped into the bottom of the cars. The picture was taken at Svartoen, on the Gulf of Bothnia.

Hold-ups like this are serious on the 'Ore Line' because the maintenance of a steady flow of ore trains to Narvik is vital; one can sometimes see as many as 20 ships at once in the harbour, queuing for their turn at the ore quays. The fact that the railway is single track may make blockages difficult to clear; in our case, for example, it was impossible to take the breakdown train to the wreck until the passengers from our train had been removed. But such emergencies are very quickly countered because of the great number of railwaymen who live along the line and who are always on call to meet them. Although this accident had only happened an hour before our arrival, news had reached Abisko and, despite the early hour, about fifty men were waiting to travel on our train to the

occurrence. A herd of about 300 reindeer was crossing the line – and in Lapland they have first priority.

Within Sweden the 'Ore Line', of course, is part of Swedish State Railways. There are only seven million people in Sweden and with 14 miles of line per 10,000 inhabitants they claim to have more railway per head of population than any other country in Europe. Originally many of the lines were privately owned, but by 1950 all but 7 per cent had been nationalized and 85 per cent of all traffic is run on electrified lines. One system of electricity is used throughout the whole country irrespective of traffic density – 16,000 volts single-phase a.c. overhead current at $16\frac{2}{3}$ cycles.

The railway not only makes the exploitation

★The incident near Abisko described in this article, when the author's Narvik express, seen in the background, encountered a derailment. The passengers and luggage are being transferred to a relief train on the other side of the blockage.

scene. No sooner had it stopped than a number of them started to transfer the freight, milk containers and other goods and to carry babies and prams over the rough ground; they also found time to offer cheerful help to passengers struggling with large suitcases – indeed, we were most impressed at the way in which our comfort was looked after. Six miles farther on our way to Kiruna we passed, in a siding, the breakdown train, which had covered the 50 miles from its base and was ready to move in as soon as we were clear.

Incidentally, novel railway experiences for the day were not quite over. Our train was speeding along trying to make up lost time when suddenly the brakes were applied and we came to a stop. This time the local people were quite unperturbed at what was, to them, an everyday

of the ore fields possible and profitable; it also is the vital artery on which the lives of the mining communities depend. Kiruna has a population of 15,000 and everything that makes life possible in such a cold remote place must come from the south by train. There is a road as far as Kiruna but it is not in any condition to carry any quantity of freight traffic. No gardening is possible there and fruit, vegetables and milk are brought by train each day from 300 or 400 miles away. The non-arrival of the milk van is a major disaster – as we saw one day when it was inadvertently left behind at Boden; long queues quickly formed at the milk shops and there were many anxious discussions before the missing van turned up at the rear of a freight train.

(Continued on page 80)

# MOTIVE POWER OF THE KIRUNA-NARVIK LINE

★One of the earlier Class 'Of' locomotives of the Kiruna–Narvik line, in its original 1-C+C-1 arrangement; as mentioned below these locomotives have since been converted into triple units. The photograph was taken near Björkliden.

## THE CLASS 'DM' LOCOMOTIVES

THE most recent type of electric locomotive developed by the Swedish State Railways for the Kiruna–Narvik ore traffic is the Class 'Dm'. The original twin-unit articulated locomotives of this type were required by specification to be able to start a train of 3,100 tons on a gradient of 1 in 100, and in conditions of snow several metres deep and temperatures as low as −40 deg. C. The main contractor was A.S.E.A., and the mechanical parts were supplied by A/B Svenska Järnvägsverkstäderna, A/B Motala Verkstad and Nydqvist & Holm A/B. The same type of locomotive has been supplied to the Norwegian State Railways under the designation 'El 12'.

The original wheel arrangement was 1−D+D−1, with side-rod drive, and the locomotive's one-hour rating 5,000 h.p. The section of the underframe between the second and third driving axle was occupied by a cast-steel motor housing which also served as a transverse connection between the frame plates. The motor housing took the bearings for the common jackshaft, which was driven by two 920-kW., series-connected motors and from which the coupling rods then transferred the driving force to the wheels. The two outer driving axles were laterally rigid; the two inner ones had ±30 mm. lateral play.

When automatic air brakes were introduced in

Sweden, the driver's brake valve then in use did not allow the driver to reduce the braking force gradually. For this reason the ore wagons were fitted with an auxiliary brake pipe to which the air from all brake cylinders escaped when the brake was released. The only communication between this auxiliary brake pipe and the atmosphere was through an auxiliary brake valve in the cab, thus permitting gradual release of the brakes. This method of operation remains in use.

Because of climatic conditions and ever-growing demands on the capacity of the line it was recently decided to increase the power of the 'Dm' locomotive to 7,500 h.p. by inserting a new unit between the two halves of the existing locomotive and thus to make the wheel arrangement 1 − D+D+D − 1. An order for this conversion was placed with the original manufacturer and the extended locomotives are now in service. They are known as Class 'Dm3'. Each locomotive is 115 ft 8 in. long and weighs 227 tons in working order, with a maximum axle load of 20 tons; it is capable of working a 4,700-ton load up a gradient of 1 in 100. The employment of these rebuilds and the introduction of new wagons is enabling the capacity of the line to be increased from the previous 13 million tons annually to between 15 and 20 million tons. A similar alteration was made some time ago to the older 'Of' class locomotives, of 1−C+C−1 arrangement; in this case three double units have been converted to two triple locomotives.

★The Norwegian version of the Swedish State Railways Class 'DM' locomotives on an ore train at Abisko. The Norwegian State Railways classify this type as 'El 12' and paint the units bright green.

★An ore train headed by one of the Class 'DM' locomotives in its original twin-unit form passes the tourist hotel at Riksgransen, on the border between Sweden and Norway. This is a very popular tourist area in summer.

★The latest triple-unit 1D+D+D1 version of Class 'Dm', with an output of 7,500 h.p.

★The Stockholm express before departure from Narvik, headed by electric locomotive No. 444.

(*Continued from page* 77)

The Kiruna mines produce 30,000 tons of high grade ore each day and 90 per cent of this goes to Narvik. At present the working is open-cast, but soon it will be entirely underground. The rock is blasted out and loaded into wagons running on standard gauge lines and drawn by electric locomotives powered from overhead wires; as soon as a fresh blast has been fired gangs of men move in to extend the line and the overhead wires up to the new ore face. The ore is dropped through crushers and passes straight from them into steel wagons each holding 40 tons, which are made up into trains of seventy wagons. Almost every hour, day and night, an ore train leaves for Narvik with 2,800 tons of the mineral. Since the wagons are con-tinuously braked, the trains move at a good pace. They are surprisingly silent and I have often been startled, when walking along the line – as one does in the wilds – suddenly to find one of these monstrous trains, nearly a quarter of a mile long, almost at my back and making speed for Narvik. The ore trains have no guard's van; instead a long pole painted red and white sticks up from the last wagon to identify it as such. After it has passed, complete silence descends once more; and there is nothing to be seen of man's activities except the one

slender line winding its way towards the hills.

Not infrequently, an ore train will be followed by an engineer's car. These are Swedish Volvo motor-cars fitted with railway wheels and a special gearbox which enables them to travel in either direction at very high speeds. They look very queer travelling backwards at speeds of up to 60 m.p.h., carrying three or four engineers facing the opposite direction. One of the railway engineers told me that the Volvos are very efficient and greatly valued for the speed with which they can get relief to any spot where there is trouble. The railway workers also make a great deal of use of tricycles. These rather unwieldy-looking devices are to be seen at many points along the line and at any station there may be over a dozen. They are essentially a bicycle, with a wheeled outrigger which runs on the second rail. They are easily lifted on to the lines by one man and, in spite of their clumsy appearance, make very good speeds.

Since there is only a single track it is quite a feat to keep a steady flow of loaded and empty ore trains and, at the same time, to cope with a considerable passenger traffic. This is achieved by having at least three places where there are a number of sidings each capable of holding a complete train. It cannot have been easy to provide these passing places, because the great size of the trains demands a very large area of level land for the sidings. A typical example is Abisko, half-way to Narvik, where it is possible to sidetrack five or six trains simultaneously and leave the main line open for through passenger traffic. It is a very impressive sight to see a number of ore trains lined up here waiting for the right away. The signalling and points are electrically controlled from a C.T.C. installation in the station building.

In summer operation may appear trouble-free, but this traffic must be maintained through the long Arctic winter, when the difficulties must be formidable. There are signs of readiness to meet emergencies everywhere. At Kiruna we counted over fifty snowploughs of various types. Along the line snow fences are built in strategic places and there are many protective snow-sheds, in which emergency equipment is stored and there are telephones, as already mentioned. Railwaymen's cottages dot the landscape every few hundred yards. As a result of all these precautions, we were told, trains are never held up, even under the most severe conditions, for more than twelve hours; and even that is exceptional. Nevertheless, before the end of the winter the line runs between walls of snow sometimes 20 ft high; they form a canyon just wide enough to admit the trains, which are

preceded by a snowplough. At these times the reindeer are one of the worst hazards. Herds of the beasts wander on to the line and, when a train comes along, they have no escape up the snow walls. The slaughter can be tremendous. When a herd of reindeer has been cut up it is the duty of the train crew to kill all the badly injured beasts; hence axes and knives are part of their equipment. Sometimes the dead animals will number over a hundred. The Government pays thousands of pounds each year to compensate the Lapp owners for this havoc, as the reindeer are their one source of livelihood.

The tremendous value of this line to the economy of Sweden can be imagined by the fact that each year the mining company of Kiruna pays over £5 million in freight charges; in consequence, this Luleå–Narvik line is by far the most profitable of all those owned by Swedish State Railways. However, it must not be forgotten that a most efficient passenger service is superimposed on the essential freight traffic. The route from Stockholm to Narvik, nearly 1,000 miles long, is a very important link in the Swedish travel service and, perhaps surprisingly, is well patronized by Norwegian businessmen. The latter have no direct line to the north of Norway and this means that, apart from flying, the quickest way of getting to such important places as Tromsø, Hammerfest and Kirkenes is to travel by train to Narvik and continue north from there by steamer or bus on the coastal road. The journey of 985 miles from Stockholm is covered in perfect comfort in just over 24 hr. In summer there are four through trains each way each day, two of them bearing names. One is called the 'Midnattsolen' (Midnight Sun), the other the 'Nordpilen' (Northern Arrow). The latter train leaves Stockholm Central Station at 5 p.m. each day, powered usually by two locomotives and loading to as many as 16 coaches. At the front there are three or four sleeping cars, the rest of the train being made up of first and second class accommodation, with either a buffet or dining car and one first class saloon fitted with easy chairs. It might be added that Swedish trains on long-distance journeys always have special accommodation for mothers and children.

The sleeping cars are excellently appointed and in all the new ones the only difference between first class and second is that the second class compartments take three passengers and the first class only two. If one has booked a sleeper, one has the use of the compartment,

★An engineer's car, a flanged-wheel version of a popular Swedish make, used extensively for fast travel to emergencies and for surveying.

which is convertible, for the whole journey. By day the seats are comfortable and in the evening women join the train and make up the beds.

It is a fascinating journey from Stockholm to Narvik because one can study the gradual change in the vegetation hour by hour as the train rushes steadily north. By 3 a.m. the train is so far north that it is broad daylight and it is often possible to look out from one's bed and see the first reindeer. Breakfast is served at 9 a.m. and by the time it is finished the train is running into the important junction and military town of Boden, 700 miles from Stockholm. Part of the train is detached here to go to Luleå, and after a break of twenty minutes the 'Nordpilen' heads in a north-westerly direction to travel right across northern Sweden and Norway. Now the trees rapidly become smaller. Within 60 more miles the engine slows to a walking pace and heralds the crossing of the Arctic Circle with fierce blasts on its whistle. The Circle crossing is marked by a line of white stones, some Lapp huts and a large board which announces the fact that the 'Land of the Midnight Sun' has been reached. Within a few hundred yards of the Circle the train stops at the unique station called Polcirkeln. It is small and very neatly kept and, although the summer only lasts eight weeks, there is a tiny lawn and flower beds gay with summer plants.

Fifty miles beyond Polcirkeln is the first of the iron ore towns. This is Gällivare, scene of the oldest workings. Now it is a large modern town with fine shops and good amenities for the thousands of people who live there. Gällivare is a railway junction, too, for the main line is joined here by the very interesting line which runs right up the centre of Sweden parallel with the main line (the latter has followed roughly the east coast) from Oestersund, on the line from Sweden to Trondheim in Norway. Until the late 1940s wood-burning locomotives were used on this line, which is not electrified, but it is now operated by smart yellow diesel cars. The journey from Oestersund, a distance of 300 miles, takes 12 hr, including two stops for meals, and runs through the heart of Lapland. The route is not easy, because all the rivers in Sweden flow to the east; in consequence this line spends its time either climbing watersheds or plunging down into the steep valleys, from each of which it must climb out. *En route* it passes through Jokkmokk, where the Lapps

have their great annual fair, and (not far from Gällivare) Harspranget and Porjus, two of the greatest hydro-electric schemes in the world, from which Sweden gets a large proportion of its electricity. From several junctions along the route short branches connect with the main coast line.

After leaving Gällivare the line climbs gently to the highest point on the Swedish State Railways at Fjallasen, 1,700 ft above sea-level. The conifer trees have now disappeared and by Kiruna only stunted birches can be seen, together with masses of bright flowers. Kiruna is a place of surprises. After many hours of travel through barren land the train suddenly enters a large modern station, its windows decorated with brightly coloured awnings, and its platforms embellished with many flower beds; nearby is a smart railway hotel and, standing in groups amongst the other passengers, there are usually a number of Lapps in their famous costume.

Kiruna mines are separated from the town by a small lake. A railway causeway has been built across an arm of it so that the ore trains can run straight from the mines on to the main line. The railway installations extend for nearly two miles. At the end of the marshalling yards there is a halt, between which and the main station a small railcar plies every 10 min., chiefly for the use of the hundreds of railway workers; but any member of the public can use it as often as he wishes – and free of charge, what is more. Incidentally, until a year or so ago Kiruna had free trams as well.

The Stockholm train's dining car is detached at Kiruna before it starts the long climb to the Norwegian border. Lapp villages with their huts and tents and reindeer herds can now be seen at many points and soon the great lakes with their splendid (but cheap) holiday hotels come into view. The train stops frequently to let passengers alight at these resorts, where they come to walk, fish, shoot, boat, paint (every other person seems to be an artist), study the Lapps, climb the mountains and enjoy the midnight sun. Soon Riksgransen (meaning 'state boundary') is reached; here the customs men come aboard and check your luggage, change your money and politely wish you a happy journey. Then the wonderful descent from the heights commences and all too soon the journey ends at Narvik.

# The South Eastern & Chatham in 1907

## by A. F. WALLIS

★ Ex-L.C.&D. Class 'M3' 4-4-0 No. 485 pulls out of Cannon Street with an express. On the left is a Class 'H' 0-4-4T on local train for Dartford via Sidcup, on the right a Class 'QI' 0-4-4T (rebuilt from a Stirling Class 'Q' 0-4-4T) leaving with a local for Dartford via Greenwich.

● A retired railwayman recalls the picturesque Edwardian days of railways in the South-East of England.

MY earliest years were spent in the environment of the South Eastern & Chatham Railway. Perhaps it would be more correct to say South Eastern Railway, because it was in the area around London Bridge that railways first entered into my bloodstream. To a certain extent the South Eastern shared with the London Brighton & South Coast Railway my interest and my loyalties, for the latter was a next-door neighbour and it was in L.B.S.C.R. employ that later I began to earn my living. Before that eventful day, however, I saw much of the S.E.C.R. and travelled over most of its main and suburban routes, with the exception of the Redhill–Reading line. I can remember the S.E.R. before its association with the London, Chatham & Dover in the Joint Managing Committee of 1899, and recall vividly the comments and speculations bandied about by those whose fortunes would be bound up with the proposed alliance. Equally vivid, in my mind at any rate, was the first appearance of the Wainwright Class 'D' and 'E' 4-4-os, with their fine brass steam domes and safety-valve seatings, the copper caps to the chimneys and the general clean, bright and smart rig-out which accompanied everything that Harry Wainwright did for the S.E.C.R.

The first seven years were indeed the formative ones for the Managing Committee, who really got down to the task of modernizing S.E.C.R. equipment, plant, operation and management as best as the stringent financial situation permitted. Therefore, it can be said that the S.E.C.R. had already turned its back upon the miserable record of the previous century, when competition in its worst form all but ruined both the South Eastern and the 'Chatham', and did nothing to further the national transport pattern that William Ewart Gladstone hoped for, and Cardwell planned. The year 1907, therefore, is selected as the frame for this article, partly because a milestone was passed in the history of the S.E.C.R., and in part because I had by that time arrived at a point when an interest in railways, and railway working, took on an aspect more serious than one normally associates with infantile delights in colourful exteriors of rolling stock.

By the summer of 1907 the new machinery had been well and truly tried, some considerable enterprise and courage had been exhibited in the construction of new and more powerful locomotives, and four major engineering operations had been finished. These were; the completion in 1904 of the complicated junctions which connected the S.E.R. at Chislehurst with the L.C.D.R. near St Mary Cray, at Bickley and at the present junction at Petts Wood; the opening on June 1, 1902, of the Bexhill branch from the Hastings main line at Crowhurst; the extension of the Chipstead Valley Line from Kingswood to Tadworth on July 1, 1900; and the opening of the Sheppey Light Railway from Queenborough to Leysdown on August 1, 1905. The last-named was acquired by the Managing Committee in the following October. The Chipstead Valley was to see a further extension to Tattenham Corner which was, however, to be used only for the Epsom race meetings. The chief of these developments was undoubtedly the Chislehurst–St Mary Cray–Bickley–Orpington spur lines that enabled trains from the S.E. section to run from the London direction to the 'Chatham' lines, and from the latter to the former, which meant that Charing Cross and Cannon Street had an alternative route to the North Kent Coast resorts than via Dartford and Strood, whilst Victoria and Holborn Viaduct enjoyed a similar facility with the Hastings and Folkestone lines of the S.E.R. The Chislehurst–St Mary Cray spur also opened up the Maidstone East line of the 'Chatham' as an alternative route to Ashford from Charing Cross or Cannon Street.

But the Chislehurst metamorphosis could not alter the pattern of the services generally, in that the consequences of the late entry of the L.C.D.R. into the London area prohibited any rationalization of the services between the one-time rival organizations. Nor did the lay-out of either enable the elimination of duplicate terminals in London, the suburbs or the country. Even today the Hastings and Folkestone line services are based upon Charing Cross or Cannon Street, and the Ramsgate via Chatham trains on Victoria, with the exception of a few morning, evening and Saturday afternoon business trains to and from the Kent Coast that use Cannon Street. Only in the extension of the Victoria/Holborn Viaduct–Bickley services to Orpington and in an experimental Victoria–Hastings service did the spur line between Bickley Junction and the present Petts Wood Junction at first serve any important function. It was not until the Continental services were resumed after the armistice of 1918, that Victoria became the London terminus for handling all boat trains to and from Dover or Folkestone.

In 1907, seven down and eight up boat train services covered the packet ports of Dover, Folkestone and Queenborough. Certain boat trains ran into and out of Cannon Street and some had Holborn Viaduct portions, which were attached to and detached from the Victoria trains at Herne Hill. The 10 a.m. from Charing Cross and the balancing inwards service, the 1.45 p.m. from Folkestone Harbour, called at Tonbridge. The 2.20 p.m. from Charing Cross had a portion for Dover (Admiralty Pier), to connect with the Ostend sailing, which was detached at Folkestone Junction before the Harbour section passed into the Junction Sidings for reversal. Both the 9 a.m. and 9 p.m. from Charing Cross made connections with Calais and Ostend sailings, whilst the 3.40 a.m. and the 3.20 p.m. from Dover did likewise with inwards services from those Continental ports. Incidentally, the 3.40 a.m. from Dover and the 11 a.m. from Victoria, with its balancing up working, the 5.20 p.m. ex-Dover, ran via Chatham, the 3.40 calling there at 4.37 a.m. To a limited extent the S.E.C.R. slipped coaches at various points, and this applied to the 9 p.m. from Charing Cross, which slipped coaches at

Shorncliffe for Folkestone Central, Folkestone Junction and Dover Town, the pre-amalgamation Dover terminus of the South Eastern. To cover weekend traffic to the Continent during the summer an extra train was run at 8.50 p.m. from Victoria to Dover (Admiralty Pier) on Fridays, to connect with the booked Calais and Ostend sailings.

The ordinary main line services were frequent enough to meet the needs of times when travel of an unessential nature was the privilege or the duty of the wealthy and higher middle classes. However, the S.E.C.R. was already beginning to build up a daily residential traffic between London and the coastal belts, which explains its substantial service of express trains. Perhaps these lost some status through the practice of working the Charing Cross trains into and out of Cannon Street, and stopping others at Herne Hill to marry the Victoria and Holborn portions or *vice versa*. Nevertheless, considering the operational problems on both the South Eastern and the Chatham sections that were associated with steep gradients, sharp curves and heavy track occupations in the London area, some really fast schedules were run, for example:

problem; despite some fast speeding down the bank, there was a passing time to be observed at Cuxton Road box, followed by the hairpin bend through Rochester. In the up direction, the foot of the bank was met immediately beyond the finish of this bend, and this, so to speak, took the stuffing out of any train booked to call at Chatham and then to run non-stop to Bromley, Herne Hill or Victoria. One of the worst hurdles to be overcome – if not the worst – was the pull out of Ramsgate Harbour immediately upon leaving the platform, in days when the allowance to Margate West without a stop at Broadstairs was 15 min. compared with 16 min. for a post-war steam timing with an additional stop at Dumpton Park. However, really fast speeds were attained in what is now described as the London area, where suburban traffic then did not attain the volume of the present day. It was not unusual to touch 60–70 m.p.h. through Hither Green in the up direction and the same could be said of the stretch between the summit at Sole Street and Farningham Road, or down the succession of short descents at the approaches to St Mary Cray, Shortlands and Herne Hill, after which

| Train | To | Arr. | Non-stop between | | Time | Distance |
|---|---|---|---|---|---|---|
| | | | | | min. | mls. ch. |
| 4.28 p.m. Charing Cross | Dover Town | 6.18 | Cannon Street | and Folkestone Centl. | 89 | 68 63 |
| 8.30 a.m. Folkestone Centl. | Charing Cross | 10.8 | Folkestone Centl. | ,, Cannon Street | 90 | 68 63 |
| 3.18 p.m. Charing Cross | Deal | 6.14 | London Bridge | ,, Ashford | 75 | 54 76 |
| 8.40 a.m. Hastings | Charing Cross | 10.26 | West St Leonard's | ,, Cannon Street | 92 | 59 51 |
| 3.25 p.m. Victoria | Ramsgate Harb. | 5.30 | Herne Hill | ,, Westgate | 93 | 68 37 |
| 5.10 p.m. Holborn Viaduct | Ramsgate Harb. | 7.2 | St Paul's | ,, Margate West | 95 | 73 0 |
| 9.50 a.m. Ramsgate Harb. | Cannon Street | 11.47 | Westgate | ,, Cannon Street | 97 | 70 14 |
| 10.0 p.m. Ramsgate Harb. | Victoria | 12.0 | Westgate | ,, Herne Hill | 90 | 68 37 |
| 5.50 p.m. Ramsgate Harb.* | Victoria | 7.50 | Margate West | ,, Herne Hill | 92 | 69 72 |
| 9.9 a.m. Victoria* | Deal | 11.17 | Herne Hill | ,, Canterbury East | 85 | 56 67 |

*Sundays

A good deal of commendable speed work was also performed over short distance, but there was no stretch of line on either section of the S.E.C.R. where fast running could be maintained for any considerable distance, except between Tonbridge and Ashford, for the whole system was beset with gradients and a galaxy of 'flat' junctions, with a number of sharp curves into the bargain. A 20 m.p.h. speed restriction applied to all Hastings line trains through the junctions at Tonbridge in either direction, although it was applicable to those routed via the Ashford line only on the Sevenoaks side of Tonbridge. Sole Street bank was a particular

more cautious running was obligatory to Victoria.

Some more interesting workings are worthy of note. For example, the 3.18 p.m. Charing Cross–Deal was the successor of the pre-1900 3.15 p.m. 'Granville Express' from Charing Cross to Ramsgate Town and Margate Sands, diverted as from Ashford to run via Folkestone; the corresponding up train, the 7.39 a.m. ex-Deal via the same route, took the place of the 9.35 a.m. ex-Margate 'Granville' to Charing Cross. There was a memory of one-time S.E.R. routing before the 'cut-off' via Chislehurst was opened, in the running of the 5.15 a.m.

'Parliamentary' train from Charing Cross to Dover Town, which called at all stations from East Croydon, and in the 8.30 a.m. from Charing Cross to Dover Town, which stopped at East Croydon, Purley, Redhill, Tonbridge, Ashford and thence all stations. In the up direction there was a mail train at 1.45 a.m. from Dover Town, calling at Folkestone Junction, Staplehurst and Tonbridge, then running fast to Cannon Street where it terminated. In those days Cannon Street was the London terminus which handled all G.P.O. traffic via the S.E.C.R. The 1.40 p.m. up from Margate Sands and the 2.25 p.m. from Dover Town travelled via Redhill, and two other unusual routings involved the 7.5 a.m. ex-Ramsgate and the 11.20 a.m. Ramsgate Harbour–Charing Cross, running via Strood and the Dartford

panies. With the G.W.R. it exchanged trains via Redhill, Guildford and Reading, and also, as with the L.N.W.R. and M.R., via the London exchange junctions. From Deal at 10.25 a.m. there ran a train for Victoria with portions for Manchester London Road, Birkenhead, Bradford and Manchester Central, which went by way of Folkestone, Tonbridge, Orpington, and dropped its 'foreign' sections at Herne Hill; the Manchester London Road and Birkenhead portions left Herne Hill at 1.5 p.m. and those for the Midland Railway at 1.10. At Kensington the Manchester London Road and Birkenhead portions parted company. The Birkenhead coach was worked specially to Ealing, where it became part of a Paddington–Birkenhead train, which in those days had to travel via Oxford because the Bicester 'cut-off' had not yet been

★The S.E.C.R. Class 'P' 0-6-0T was designed primarily for light branch and rail-motor service of the kind illustrated here. Formations of this kind were operating between Nunhead Junction and Greenwich Park (seen here), Otford and Sevenoaks, and Reading and Ash.

Loop. A measure of rationalization of the main line services between the London termini of the South Eastern and the Chatham Section had already taken place by 1907, for few trains for Ramsgate and Margate still followed the former Tonbridge route, and not many for Dover ran via Chatham. Late evening facilities from London included an 11.45 p.m. from Charing Cross to Tunbridge Wells, and a 12 midnight from Charing Cross to Ramsgate Harbour, calling only at Whitstable, Herne Bay, Westgate and then all station, which ran on Wednesdays and Saturdays respectively.

The S.E.C.R. built up two most useful through services with the Great Western, London & North Western and Midland com-

opened; the Manchester London Road vehicles were attached to the 'Sunny South Special' which had come up from Eastbourne via Brighton. The Midland coaches proceeded over the Metropolitan Widened Lines and Kings Cross Junction to Hendon, but the Bradford and Manchester Central sections were not separated before Leicester, where they were attached to trains from St Pancras. S.E.C.R. engines were responsible for working the through coaches as far as Kensington and Hendon. The guards also came from the S.E.C.R. To cover the possibility of late running from the south into Hendon – and there was a very short margin before the balancing train arrived from the north – a 'conditional' stop at Kentish Town was embodied in the working timetable so that the guards could change over.

The remaining S.E.C.R. main line services of the period included semi-fast and all-stations stopping trains to and from the coastal termini and intermediate stations of importance such as Tonbridge, Ashford (via Maidstone East), Sheerness, Gillingham and Faversham. Services routed via Croydon for the Redhill and Oxted lines had to share paths with L.B.S.C.R. trains as far as Redhill, but ever since the opening of the shorter route to Tonbridge via Chislehurst in 1868, the Redhill–Tonbridge line had lost much of its main line status. For a long time the practice of combining Tonbridge and Reading portions as far as Redhill had been much in evidence. Oxted line trains usually terminated there, but a few were extended to Eden-bridge or Tonbridge via the junctions near Crowhurst. For the Caterham and Chipstead Valley lines a shuttle service was operated from and to Purley in connection with Redhill trains, but during the busy periods of the day a few ran between both branches and Charing Cross or Cannon Street. There were a few fast business trains in the mornings and in the evenings which were booked non-stop between London Bridge and Redhill or Coulsdon & Cane Hill (now Coulsdon South); some of

these terminated at Dorking and Gomshall.

Branch line services, generally, were integrated with those operating along the main lines in good connections at junctions. But there was, and always will be, a problem to make such connections universally convenient, especially where a branch runs from one main line to another – for example, at Paddock Wood at one end and at Strood at the opposite. With the exception of the Elham Valley line, most of the services 'shuttled' between the junction and the end of the branch, especially where the latter was a dead-end. The Elham Valley trains operated in clockwise and anti-clockwise fashion; thus the 1.26 p.m. Margate–Dover Harbour, via Minster and Deal, formed the 2.47 p.m. Dover Harbour–Margate via Folke-stone, Elham Valley line, Canterbury West and Minster, due back at Margate at 4.59. The anti-clockwise style was exemplified by the 7.50 p.m. Margate–Dover Harbour, via Minster, Canter-bury West and Elham Valley, which formed the 10 p.m. Dover Harbour–Margate, via Deal and Minster. At this stage, the spur line between Sandwich and Ramsgate, which avoids running into and out of Minster, was laid in, but not used for passenger traffic. Mondays to Fridays, the day's work on each of the country branches in 1907 was:

| Branch | Operated between | | Total trains | Approximate journey time |
|---|---|---|---|---|
| | a.m. | p.m.* | | min. |
| Ashford–Margate        .    .    .    .    . | 6.40 | 11.34 | 26 | 90 |
| Canterbury–Whitstable  .    .    .    .    . | 7.30 | 9.30 | 21 | 15 |
| Minster–Deal .    .    .    .    .    .    . | 6.42 | 10.45 | 30 | 15–19 |
| Elham Valley .    .    .    .    .    .    . | 7.30 | 9.30 | 16 | |
| Sandgate–Sandling Junction    .    .    .    . | 7.20 | 9.44 | 34 | ⎰10 (Down) ⎱13 (Up) |
| Ashford–Hastings  .    .    .    .    .    . | 6.45 | 10.34 | 27 | 60 |
| New Romney–Appledore   .    .    .    .    . | 6.45 | 9.25 | 19 | 26 |
| Dungeness–Lydd    .    .    .    .    .    . | 7.40 | 5.54 | 8 | 10 |
| Bexhill–Crowhurst .    .    .    .    .    . | 7.5 | 9.28 | 32 | 10 |
| Hawkhurst–Paddock Wood  .    .    .    .    . | 7.9 | 10.25 | 20 | 25–28 |
| Paddock Wood–Maidstone  .    .    .    .    . | 6.25 | 11.55 | 20 | 25–28 |
| Hundred of Hoo†   .    .    .    .    .    . | 7.50 | 9.25 | 12 | 45–57 |
| Sheerness–Sittingbourne .    .    .    .    . | 6.35 | 10.15 | 18 | 25 |
| Sheppey (Queenborough–Leysdown)   .    .    . | 7.0 | 8.3 | 14 | 33 |
| Dover–Deal .    .    .    .    .    .    .    . | 7.20 | 11.8 | 27 | 25 |
| Kearnsey–Deal .    .    .    .    .    .    . | 7.23 | 10.39 | 14 | 20 |
| Gravesend (West Street) .    .    .    .    . | 8.8 | 10.39 | 14 | 24 |
| Westerham–Dunton Green  .    .    .    .    . | 6.25 | 12.57 a.m. | 26 | 11 |
| Ash–Aldershot .    .    .    .    .    .    . | 7.30 | 12.11 a.m. | 42 | 5 |

* The times shown in this column represent in each case the time of arrival at destination of the last train over the branch.
† Gravesend Central–Port Victoria.

There were, of course, later trains on Wednesdays or Thursdays to coincide with the mid-week early closing of shops, whilst on Saturdays and Sundays a similar facility was also provided in districts where the volume of traffic justified it. Certain trains originating at the head of a branch ran beyond the junction station – for example, the 8.53 a.m. from Bexhill, after calling at Sidley, made Tunbridge Wells the only stop before reaching Cannon Street at 10.37; and the 8.8 a.m. from Gravesend (West Street) was one of three that went through to Victoria, with a similar operation taking place in the opposite direction (otherwise, the general practice was to terminate and start the branch services at Swanley Junction where better run-round facilities were available than at Farningham Road). On weekdays (except Thursdays) during the summer a steam railcar unit operated a Sandgate–Dover Town service, occupying 45 min. on a journey that included reversal at Sandling Junction. The total of 42 trains per day for the Ash–Aldershot service may seem liberal, but it should be borne in mind that the short spur between the S.E.C.R. and the L.S.W.R. systems brought the former into the principal Aldershot station of the latter, and, as this was more central than the North Camp station of the S.E.C.R., a considerable amount of military personnel would be carried.

Suburban services were sufficiently various and frequent to justify an article to themselves, but in general they followed the present-day pattern, with the following differences:

| 1907 service | Present-day equivalent |
| --- | --- |
| Woodside to Selsdon Road | Cannon Street to Sanderstead, via Mid-Kent line |
| Beckenham Junction to Crystal Palace (Low Level) | Beckenham Junction to Victoria, via Crystal Palace and Balham |
| Victoria and Holborn Viaduct to Crystal Palace (High Level) | |
| Nunhead to Greenwich Park | |
| Beckenham Junction to Norwood Junction | *Withdrawn* |
| Victoria to Moorgate Street, via Loughborough Junction and Snow Hill | |
| Ludgate Hill to Wimbledon, via Tulse Hill and Tooting (L.S.W.R.) trains | Holborn Viaduct to West Croydon, via Tulse Hill, Wimbledon and St Helier |

The Woodside–Selsdon Road, the Beckenham Junction–Norwood Junction and the Beckenham Junction–Crystal Palace services were covered by steam railcars, the journey time taking 11, 5 and 10 min. respectively; they operated on weekdays only and were infrequent – 20 workings both ways on the Crystal Palace, and 17 on the Norwood Junction service. As the Woodside–Selsdon Road trains made connections with the Addiscombe Road trains from and to London, and as far as possible did the same with the Croydon & Oxted Joint Line at Selsdon Road, this had a total of 16 or 17 trains each way. The line between Woodside and Selsdon Road, being the joint property of the L.B.S.C.R. and S.E.C.R., was operated and staffed by the latter undertaking, although the Croydon & Oxted, also under a joint ownership, was the responsibility of the 'Brighton' throughout, except at Upper Warlingham.

A service between Victoria and Moorgate Street was operated throughout the day from about 6.30 a.m. to 11.30 p.m., with earlier trains to Holborn Viaduct only Certain trains terminated at Snow Hill (now shown in the working timetables as Holborn Low Level), some at Ludgate Hill and a few at St Paul's. A few ran between Moorgate Street and Clapham Junction, L.S.W.R., via Longhedge, a route that was followed by a series of trains operated by the L.S.W.R. between Ludgate Hill and Richmond, via Kensington, Hammersmith, Studland Road and Gunnersbury, in addition to a Ludgate Hill–Wimbledon service, which employed the loops via Haydons Road and via Merton Abbey between Tooting Junction and Wimbledon. The journey times were: Victoria–Moorgate, 38 min.; Clapham Junction–Moorgate, 36 min.; Ludgate Hill–Richmond, 60 min. and Ludgate Hill–Wimbledon, 32 min. The Midland company was still operating its Hendon–Victoria services with its own rolling stock and engines, and the G.N.R. the same with the through trains from Finsbury Park and beyond to Woolwich, via Blackfriars, London Bridge and Blackheath.

At the time of fusion of the S.E.R. and L.C.D.R. adequate motive power for express traffic was lacking. A few S.E.R. Class 'B' and L.C.D.R. Class 'M' 4-4-0s were the only really up-to-date locomotives available. This situation Wainwright soon began to rectify by embarking upon drastic rebuilding of the ex-S.E.R. Classes 'F' and 'Q' and by introducing more powerful 4-4-0s in the

**Right:** With brass dome gleaming, Wainwright Class 'E' 4-4-0 No. 19, built in 1908 with extended smokebox, heads a down express near Grove Park.

**Below:** A James Stirling Class 'F' 4-4-0, also near Grove Park, on a train of mixed rolling stock which includes as its

second vehicle one of the first bogie coaches to operate in the south of England; this vehicle was built by R. C. Mansell in 1879.

**Right:** A Class 'D' and a Class 'B' 4-4-0 double-head a Continental express including Pullman cars south of Hither Green.

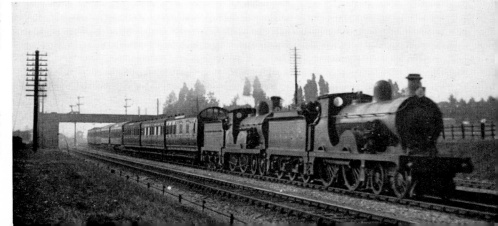

★The postal sorting vans which Wainwright built at Ashford survived until the final days of steam on the South Eastern Division of the Southern Region. They are seen above in the 9 a.m. Continental Mail of the S.E.C.R., photographed near Grove Park behind Class 'E' 4-4-0 No. 165; and below, in December, 1958, as the second and third vehicles of this Christmas mail train for Ramsgate photographed at Minster East Junction behind Class 'D1' 4-4-0 No. 31739.

[Below: M. R. Galley

shape of Classes 'D' and 'E'. For suburban traffic he turned out the Class 'H' and 'R' 0-4-4Ts. The new Class 'D' and 'E' 4-4-0s covered all the boat trains between Charing Cross and Victoria and Folkestone and Dover, while the ex-L.C.D.R. Class 'M' 4-4-0s looked after the Queenborough services. The 'Ds' and 'Es' also managed the express work

from Charing Cross or Cannon Street to the Folkestone and Hastings lines, while the 'Ms' shared with a few Class 'Ds' the Victoria–Ramsgate Harbour express trains; the 'Ms' were also to be found on the Chatham Section excursion work from Victoria. The S.E.R. Classes 'B' and 'F' catered for all the semi-fast and stopping train work on their home section, including the Redhill line trains; individual engines were withdrawn for reconditioning as operating circumstances allowed.

As much S.E. Section suburban work as possible was rostered for the 'Q' class (whether rebuilt or not) until the Class 'H' 0-4-4Ts gradually took over their duties. On the Chatham Section the ex-L.C.D.R. Class 'A' 0-4-4Ts did yeoman service on the trains run from Victoria or Holborn via Herne Hill and Nunhead, and on the Victoria–Moorgate services. The Pickersgill 4-4-0s originally built for the Great North of Scotland Railway also did useful work on the semi-fast services and slower long-distance trains over the North Kent line to Chatham and beyond

During 1907 a number of corridor carriages with vestibule connections were under construction at Ashford works for the through services to and from the provincial towns on the Great Western, London & North Western and Midland systems. Some of them found their way into boat train and other express train formations. To suit their principal function as through coaches, many of these vehicles were brake composites comprising two first and three third class compartments. The South Eastern 'birdcage', with the four windows at the extreme end of the guard's-cum-luggage compartment, was employed; it had a seat for the guard set at one end of a raised platform. Four of these carriages, Nos. 913–916, passed into Southern Railway stock in 1923 and were eventually numbered 6622–6625. In every way the outward appearance of the trains showed a marked improvement, down to such detail as the red roofboards with gilt lettering of the express formations.

Talking of these, the legend 'Continental Mail Express' regularly appeared on the roofboards of the Charing Cross–Dover boat trains because they invariably carried the Continental G.P.O. mails, and sorting vans were included in the 9 p.m. from Charing Cross and the 3.40 a.m. from Dover. For these two night Continental mail trains, Wainwright built at Ashford some postal sorting vans that were

attached and detached at Cannon Street. They carried on each side the words 'Royal Mail – Malle Royale' above the royal coat-of-arms at the waist line, but otherwise were painted in the standard S.E.C.R. livery. The vans did not carry any pick-up apparatus but they were vestibuled; two were usually run in one train formation. These vans were still in service in the 1950s on the 11.50 p.m. London Bridge–Deal via Redhill and Dover, Mondays to Saturdays, and 9.5 p.m. on Sundays; also on the 9.28 p.m. Margate–London Bridge via Dover and Redhill every weekday, or 9.20 p.m. on Sundays.

The most picturesque train sets were those of the 3.35 p.m. Charing Cross–Hastings and 4.28 p.m. Charing Cross–Dover 'American Car' trains and their balancing up services, the 8.40 a.m. from Hastings and the 8.30 a.m. from Folkestone Central. Their coaches were constructed in 1896 for the former S.E.R. in the Pullman style, with four-wheeled bogies and Gould automatic couplers. Finished externally in the new S.E.C.R. livery with 'SOUTH EASTERN & CHATHAM RAILWAY' wrought in gold leaf along the panel immediately below the roof, they had an elaborate internal decor, with movable armchairs, that savoured of the Victorian era. Despite such 'extras' as separate toilets for ladies, Baker's hot water and Stone's electric lighting systems, no supplementary fares were charged on the 'American Car' trains.

There were some tri-composites with brake ends, but owing to the exceptional amount of seating room allowed in the first class, which accommodated only four per compartment, against six in the second, and 12 in the third, total seating did not exceed 26 per vehicle. When formed into the 10.25 a.m. ex-Deal, these vehicles added to the variety of Midland 'red', L.N.W.R. dark chocolate and white and G.W.R. pale chocolate and cream. Otherwise, main line and boat trains had separate coaches for first, second and third class travellers – although there were relatively few third class passengers to be found on the Continental services, and certainly none at all on those operated via Folkestone, or on the 11 a.m. and 5.20 p.m. ex-Victoria and Dover Admiralty Pier respectively. Gradually, new three-coach units were drafted on to the main line and subsidiary line services and many of them were still to be seen in early B.R. days on the Tonbridge–Redhill–Reading trains and on the cross-country route between Tonbridge and

★Stirling Class 'B' 4-4-0 No. 458, built in 1898; this was one of two which retained their original domeless boilers.

★Stirling Class 'A' 4-4-0 No. 175, built in 1881 and withdrawn in 1908.

★No. 679 was one of five 4-4-0s originally ordered from Neilsons for the Great North of Scotland Railway, but which were sold new to the S.E.C.R.

★Stirling 4-4-0 No. 217 after rebuilding by Wainwright from Class 'B' to 'B1', but before fitting with extended smokebox in Maunsell's day.

★Class 'E' 4-4-0 No. 273, the prototype of the class.

★Class 'M3' 4-4-0 No. 476 was an L.C.D.R. type.

Brighton via Tunbridge Wells, Uckfield and Lewes.

In 1907 suburban rolling stock included a number of ex-S.E.R. and ex-L.C.D.R. carriages for all three classes of travel. Whilst the 1899-built South Eastern four-wheeler first and second class composites (two compartments of each) could not be called old, many of the third class coaches still had the low-back seats from which the occupants could see all that was going on and hear all that was said by fellow travellers in the next compartment. New suburban trains of six-wheelers were constructed, but not enough to eliminate some engaging makeshifts from time to time in the carriage workings. For instance, the stock of the 10 a.m. Charing Cross–Folkestone boat train would be used occasionally for the 8.37 a.m. from Hayes, giving suburban passengers the luxury of corridor stock for their morning journey to town.

Experiments were undertaken with steam railcars on certain branches, such as the Beckenham–Crystal Palace and Beckenham–Norwood Junction lines, and on the Sandgate–Dover Town service, which involved reversal at Sandling Junction. Rail-motors had been in vogue on other railways in this country before the S.E.C.R. introduced in 1906 a 38-ton unit, fitted with a 0-4-0T engine of a special Wainwright design. The locomotive portions were built by Kitsons of Leeds and were detachable; the coach bodies were constructed by a number of builders.

The S.E.C.R. was not slow to exploit its seaside resorts from Sheerness to Bexhill, and the delightful countryside on the edge of London. Here are some examples of the concessionary fares that were available at this period:

● London to Hythe, Sandgate, Folkestone, Dover, Deal, Canterbury, Ramsgate, Margate, St Leonard's, Bexhill: **4s. day excursion.**
● London to Boulogne: **12s. 6d. day excursion.**
● Victoria to Whitstable and Herne Bay: **2s. 6d. half-day excursion.**
● New Cross, Forest Hill, Norwood Junction and East Croydon to Folkestone and Dover: **2s. 6d., 2s. 9d., 3s. 3d., 3s. 6d. respectively, half-day excursion**
● Oxted–Tunbridge Wells: **1s. 9d. day excursion.**
● Abbey Wood to Woolwich Arsenal: **market ticket 3d. return.**
● Sunday in Paris – out by night service from Charing Cross on Saturday, return Sunday by night service from Paris: **45s., 27s. 6d. and 20s.** first, second and third class respectively.

● **Holiday tickets – 7s. return,** available for one or two weeks from London stations to all coastal resorts; or **10s. return,** available for one month from London to all coastal resorts – outward and return journeys to be undertaken on Thursdays and Saturdays respectively.
● **Rail and steamboat tickets** – available by either means of transport, provided either the rail or the steamer was used for the outward journey – Ramsgate to Folkestone: **4s.;** Dover: **3s.;** and Deal: **1s. 6d. return.**:

A number of combined return tickets were issued from the London stations to Southend, Ramsgate and Margate, available in one direction by the General Steam Navigation Co.'s 'Eagle' steamers which served Ramsgate and Margate. Where Southend was concerned, the tickets were available by the Medway Steam Packet Co.'s sailings between Chatham (Sun Pier) and Southend.

Engineering works that were completed by 1907 included, besides the series of spur lines near Chislehurst, the widening of the tracks between London Bridge and Orpington, incorporating an additional tunnel at Elmstead Woods. Spa Road station was enlarged and a new one was built at Southwark Park (between Spa Road and North Kent East Junction); additionally, stations at Hither Green, Grove Park, Chislehurst and Orpington were rebuilt. The S.E.C.R. also derived some advantage from the improvements that the L.B.S.C.R. made at East Croydon and Purley, and the relief from the congestion at Redhill when the latter company opened their Quarry line by-passing Redhill in 1900. Other works that were in full swing in 1907 included the building of a new depot at Ewer Street, Southwark, near the Borough Market, to handle the increasing Continental fruit traffic, and improvements at the waterside depots of Blackfriars and Angerstein Wharf. The electrification of the London County Council tramway systems that had been completed in South-East London by 1904 had enticed away some of the short-distance suburban traffic, but the S.E.C.R. built up compensating traffic in the Hither Green and Well Hall areas by fostering new housing estates. On the catering side, contracts of many years' standing were in force with Messrs. Spiers & Pond Ltd. in respect of South Eastern Section stations, but just prior to 1907 Messrs. Lyons & Co. secured the contract for all refreshment room catering at Chatham Section stations. The company did not possess or operate restaurant cars. Whilst on the subject of catering, it might be mentioned that the hotels at the Cannon

Street, Charing Cross, Holborn Viaduct and Victoria stations were in the hands of the Managing Committee, who also owned the palatial South Eastern Hotel on the front at Deal; special first class travel tickets were issued that included full board and accommodation at this establishment.

Continental traffic remained one of the S.E.C.R.'s principal sources of revenue and it began to grow as the first decade of the present century neared its end. At the time of the merger all the vessels on both the Calais and Boulogne routes were still paddle steamers, but by the summer of 1907 the turbine engine had come into use. At this time the fleet in regular use comprised:

| Name of vessel | Gross | Speed | Year introduced | Service |
|---|---|---|---|---|
| | tons | knots | | |
| Princess of Wales*† | 1,366 | 19 | 1897 | Folkestone–Boulogne |
| Mabel Grace* | 1,215 | 20 | 1899 | Folkestone–Boulogne |
| Calais* | 1,002 | 19 | 1896 | Dover–Calais |
| Dover* | 1,002 | 19 | 1896 | Dover–Calais |
| Lord Warden* | 1,002 | 19 | 1896 | Dover–Calais |
| The Queen | 1,676 | 21¾ | 1903 | Either |
| Onward | 1,679 | 22 | 1905 | Either |
| Invicta | 1,679 | 22 | 1905 | Either |
| Empress | 1,695 | 22½ | 1907 | Either |
| Victoria | 1,689 | 22½ | 1907 | Either |

\* Paddle steamers.
† Two bell-top funnels. The *Mabel Grace* and the five turbine vessels all had funnels of the conventional style.

Improved amenities for the passenger characterized the new turbine steamers and lessened the disagreeable nature of the crossing under adverse weather conditions. Although only a few feet in the beam distinguished them from their older sisters, the extra 40–50 lineal ft built into them helped to increase the passenger space, whilst their improved steaming ability shortened the open sea crossing. Nor was the freight-carrying side of the Continental business neglected. Between 1900 and 1907 the cargo fleet gross tonnage increased from 2,051 to 3,707 with the introduction of three new twin-screw ships – *Canterbury*, *Hythe* and *Folkestone*.

Fifty years ago the administration and operation were in the capable hands of Mr Vincent Hill, the General Manager who, up to the time of his taking over on June 1, 1901, had held a similar office on the Hull, Barnsley & West Riding Dock Co., which later became the Hull & Barnsley Railway. He was assisted by Messrs W. Thompson, the Superintendent of the Line, F. H. Dent, the Goods Manager, P. C. Tempest, the Chief Engineer, and H. S. Wainwright, the Locomotive Engineer, as chief

★Class 'A' 0-4-4T No. 567, a former L.C.D.R. type for suburban duty; it was fitted with condensing apparatus for through working to the G.N.R. via the Metropolitan Widened Lines.

officers. Mr (later Sir Francis) Dent, destined to become the General Manager, came from the London & North Western to the S.E.C.R. and brought with him Mr F. W. West, who in the capacity of London District Goods Superintendent became a leading factotum in the reconstruction of the goods services and methods of handling at the depots. To Mr (later Sir Percy) Tempest, who also became the last General Manager immediately prior to the formation of the Southern Railway, great credit was due for the many engineering schemes that have already been mentioned. Harry Wainwright's far-sighted accomplishments, in spite

★Class 'H' 0-4-4T No. 269; this was one of the early examples of a class introduced in 1904 to replace the Class 'Q' (see facing page).

★Class 'Q' 0-4-4T No. 23, a Stirling suburban tank design introduced in 1881.

of some justifiable financial restrictions, have also been discussed. As the fusion between the South Eastern and the London, Chatham & Dover companies was not a complete amalgamation in the more generally accepted meaning of the term, in addition to the Managing Committee, the respective Boards of the South Eastern and the 'Chatham' remained operative, the shareholders meeting every half-year to declare the dividends and the merits or demerits of the work accomplished during the preceding period. Mr Cosmo Bonsor presided over the South Eastern Board and Sir William Hart-Dyke over the L.C.D.R., the former being the Chairman of the Joint Managing Committee and the latter Deputy Chairman.

★Class 'O' 0-6-0 No. 394, James Stirling's first design for the S.E.R. after his appointment as that railway's Locomotive Superintendent in 1878; the 0-6-0s were very similar to a previous design of his for the Glasgow & South Western Railway.

Had it not been for the intervention of the First World War, greater and wider achievements would have been credited to the Managing Committee, including some electrification (*see following article*), and the reorganization of the lines in Thanet. This matured in 1926, when the former stations at Ramsgate Harbour, Ramsgate Town and Margate Sands were closed and the former Chatham Section line was diverted at a point east of Broadstairs to an alignment that today approaches a new Ramsgate station (near the site of the old St Lawrence), via one erected at Dumpton Park.

# The S.E.C.R. electrification schemes of 1903 and 1919

PARLIAMENTARY powers were obtained in 1903 by the South Eastern & Chatham Railway to electrify its suburban lines. In 1912 the Managing Committee consulted Messrs Merz & McLellan, Consulting Engineers, who presented their report in the following year. This recommended the conversion by stages of the whole of the suburban lines and the main lines to Hastings, Dover and Ramsgate, as well as the two Maidstone lines, the branches from Redhill to Reading and Tonbridge, and the Oxted line to Edenbridge. The estimated cost of conversion was £5,599,000, but a saving in operating cost of £350,000 a year was anticipated. The scheme budgeted for an all-round improvement of 20 per cent in speed and frequency of train service and it was expected to increase revenue in the suburban area by 50 per cent which would have amounted to a return of 20 per cent on the capital outlay.

The 1,500-volt direct current system was considered the most suitable for conditions on the S.E.C.R. Both third rail and overhead wire current collection were to be employed, but the principal means would have been third rail; the traction units' collecting shoes were to make contact with the underside of the conductor rail, the top of which was to be protected. The overhead wire was to be used in goods sorting sidings and carriage yards. All the 166 locomotives and 666 m.u. coaches were to be fitted with dual equipment. Estimates showed that although £700,000 could be saved by installing 6,000-volt single-phase a.c. power distribution, the rolling stock equipment would have cost £1,900,000 more than for the d.c. installation; moreover, adoption of the a.c. method would have added another £72,000 to the annual working expenses.

The use of electric locomotives for main line work was calculated to show several advantages, chiefly a lower cost of renewals and maintenance and a longer actual life in service. The type of passenger locomotive proposed had four driving wheels and a four-wheel bogie; for heavy trains two machines could be coupled to make up a 2 − Bo + Bo − 2 unit. For freight work an eight-wheeled machine was to be built. The suburban stock was to be composed of two-car sets with one motor-coach to each unit.

In 1919 Mr Alfred Raworth, Electrical Engineer of the S.E.C.R., prepared a fresh report on electrification, as the rise in the cost of materials and labour since the original proposals had revised the economics of main line conversion. It was now proposed to make Gillingham and Tonbridge the limits of haulage by electric locomotives of main-line passenger and goods trains. A total of 36 passenger locomotives was proposed and then were estimated to cost £7,000 each. For goods trains 50 locomotives would have been required, at £4,200 each. The cost of converting the suburban area, including the provision of locomotives and power distribution, was now estimated at £13,241,000, more than double the pre-war assessment; yet in spite of the large capital outlay, the calculations indicated that £421,943 could be saved annually by the electrification, and if the receipts in the suburban area increased by 50 per cent the net annual gain would be £1,250,000.

The conversion was to be tackled in three stages. Stage 1 comprised the Orpington, Bromley North, North Kent, Mid-Kent, Catford Loop and Crystal Palace lines. Services during both rush and slack periods were to be three trains an hour. Stage 2 envisaged extensions to Tonbridge, Caterham, Tadworth, Dorking and Edenbridge via Croydon, and Gillingham via Swanley and via Gravesend. Other lines of which electrification was contemplated were the Westerham and Gravesend West branches and the Redhill–Tonbridge line. On all the lines in Stage 2 it was proposed to run two trains an hour in peak periods, with an hourly service during the day. A schedule of 58 min. from Charing Cross to Gillingham via Gravesend, with nine intermediate stops, was contemplated, and from Victoria via Swanley the run was to be made in 62 min. with ten stops; Edenbridge would have been reached in 47 min. from Charing Cross with seven intermediate stops. Stage 3 was to effect the working of through passenger and goods trains by electric locomotives to the limits of the electrified area, where trains were to be handed over to steam locomotives.

Under the modified scheme, the suburban trains were to be formed from 193 three-car units, having two third class motor-coaches each equipped with two 200 h.p. motors, and a first class trailer-coach. Each motor-coach was to have seated 96 passengers, arranged six-a-side, and the first class coach was to have 64 seats in eight compartments. A nine-coach train would thus have had seats for 768 passengers. The coaches were to have been 9 ft wide and 57 ft long.

A generating station at Angerstein's Wharf was proposed, and four substations were to be erected at Lewisham Junction, Rochester Bridge, Redhill and Tonbridge. Here the 33,000-volt three-phase current was to have been converted to 1,500-volt d.c., and fed into two conductor rails running along each track. In sidings, overhead wires were proposed. The conductor rails were to be protected by timber to minimize the chance of accidental contact, and the running rails were to be bonded for the return current. The system proposed was believed to have been best suited to the needs of suburban and main-line working and it could have been further extended to cover all main lines and link up with the Channel Tunnel, if that were constructed.